ADVENTURES
OF THE
SOUL

ALSO BY JAMES VAN PRAAGH

Books

How to Heal a Grieving Heart (with Doreen Virtue)*
Talking to Heaven
Reaching to Heaven
Healing Grief
Heaven and Earth
Meditations with James Van Praagh
Looking Beyond
Ghosts Among Us
Unfinished Business
Growing Up in Heaven

Card Decks

*The Soul's Journey Lesson Cards**
Talking to Heaven Mediumship Cards
(with Doreen Virtue)*

Online Courses

*How to Heal a Grieving Heart**
Enhancing Your Intuition
Life After Loss
Mastering Meditation

Downloadable Meditations

Divine Love
Meditation Tools
Soul Discoveries
Spirit Speaks

*Available from Hay House

Please visit:
Hay House USA: www.hayhouse.com®
Hay House Australia: www.hayhouse.com.au
Hay House UK: www.hayhouse.co.uk
Hay House South Africa: www.hayhouse.co.za
Hay House India: www.hayhouse.co.in

James's website: www.vanpraagh.com

ADVENTURES
OF THE
SOUL

Journeys Through the Physical
and Spiritual Dimensions

James Van Praagh

HAY HOUSE, INC.
Carlsbad, California • New York City
London • Sydney • Johannesburg
Vancouver • Hong Kong • New Delhi

Published and distributed in the United States by: Hay House, Inc.: www.hayhouse.com® • *Published and distributed in Australia by:* Hay House Australia Pty. Ltd.: www.hayhouse.com.au • *Published and distributed in the United Kingdom by:* Hay House UK, Ltd.: www.hayhouse.co.uk • *Published and distributed in the Republic of South Africa by:* Hay House SA (Pty), Ltd.: www.hayhouse.co.za • *Distributed in Canada by:* Raincoast Books: www.raincoast.com • *Published in India by:* Hay House Publishers India: www.hayhouse.co.in

Cover design: Leanne Siu Anastasi • *Interior design:* Tricia Breidenthal

Cataloging-in-Publication Data is on file with the Library of Congress

Hardcover ISBN: 978-1-4019-4470-4

10 9 8 7 6 5 4 3 2 1
1st edition, September 2014

Printed in the United States of America

To Debbie Ford.
Thank you for bringing
the shadows into the light.
Love, James

CONTENTS

INTRODUCTION

Those of you who have read my previous books will find this one to be a little different.

The basis of my other books has been the thousands of readings I've done as a professional medium over the last 30 years. When my first bestseller, *Talking to Heaven,* exploded onto the scene back in 1997, the subject of talking to the dead and mediumship was not part of our cultural zeitgeist. Fast-forward to 2014, and *Ghost Whisperer* and *Medium* have aired for several seasons each, *The Sixth Sense* has been nominated for a Best Picture Oscar, the movie *Ghost* has been adapted into a Broadway musical, and other popular mediums (many of whom I count as friends) are sharing their gifts with the world.

I've stopped doing private readings now (except for the occasional charity event), and I've focused my energy on training other people to develop their own psychic gifts and—if they wish—to start on their journey to help others. I get so much satisfaction out of opening minds to the wonders of Spirit that I tour the world presenting lectures about spirituality. And, of course, during those events, I give demonstrations of my ability to make contact with the consciousnesses of those who no longer inhabit this physical dimension.

That really is what most of the people who come to my lectures want to see, but I always give them a healthy dose of what really matters: the truth that there is no "death" and that what we believe about our lives on Earth—about this being our true nature—is just an illusion. We are eternal souls that have no beginning and no end, but while we're incarnated in this physical dimension, we are only aware of *now*. The wholeness of who we really are is filtered through our human senses, so we are not capable of seeing the big picture.

As I will recount in this book, there *are* ways we can get glimpses of our true nature: through meditation, out-of-body experiences, and the accounts of near-death-experience survivors; by being regressed to past lives; and from information channeled via mediums. As a person who has been blessed with the ability to communicate with souls who have transitioned to the Spirit realms, I personally cannot deny the experiences I have had. If it wasn't happening to me, I would be skeptical, too.

If you were to ask me what I've learned from my career as a medium, it would be that the most important thing we humans can do is to utilize the energy of love. Earth is a very busy place, and we're constantly bombarded with challenges and obstacles. We are rewarded and encouraged when we separate ourselves from the pack. We are tempted to equate money or fame with success, but that is a false god. The Beatles summed it up very eloquently: *All you need is love.*

I'd like you to think of your soul as a big, long river. As it flows and meanders, sometimes it stops to pool. Think of that as an incarnation in the physical. After a while, the flow starts up again, until it reaches another pool. But there is always movement, there is always a destination, there is always growth. The river can bend and turn, but it does have an ultimate goal: to be united with the sea . . . the whole. Likewise, the mission of your soul is utilize the energy of love in order to make a successful return home to *its* Source.

My wish is that as you're reading this book, you'll come to understand that there is more to "life" than what you can perceive with your five senses. For instance, I look out at the park across the street from my home and I see the squirrels that live there. They inhabit a finite space, and it's all that they know. It is their world. The reality that there's a big planet on which they could roam is not even something they can conceive of. That possibility is not even on their radar.

In contrast, evolution has given us humans the ability to ponder other universes and other dimensions. Will it ever be possible to know the truth of why we are here while we process that question through our human brain? Have we been given another path to access the mysteries of the Universe? And is it really our purpose to know? I hope that this book will start you on your own personal quest to find these answers.

So come with me as I take you on adventures through space and time and heavenly realms that will, hopefully, lead your soul—your river—to the sea of love.

— James Van Praagh

PART I

WHAT
IS THE
SOUL?

CHAPTER ONE

BODY, SOUL, AND SPIRIT

From the beginning of time, humankind has been on a quest to understand the concept of the soul. Through the generations, theologians, scholars, philosophers, and even musicians have attempted to describe it in an easily digestible manner for us mentally driven humans to comprehend. To this day, the terms *soul* and *spirit* are used interchangeably, without the true meaning of either being accurately presented or understood.

Working as a messenger for the Spirit World for the last three decades, I have also embarked on my own quest to find the correct definition of the soul and how the soul functions. Being a teacher and a role model for others, I think that this is imperative. When I sit in meditation, teach a class, or deliver messages from the other side, I often silently inquire of my guides and visiting spirits just how we humans can come closer to understanding the nature of the soul.

It has been impressed upon me over and over again to think of it in terms of a *holy trinity*. I know that sounds religious, but I think that it's only Spirit using terminology that is already in my brain file. Since I'm not a scientist or mathematician, Spirit wouldn't be giving me formulas that I don't understand. Neither am I an engineer or a theologian. I'm just a guy from Queens who happened to be raised Catholic.

But the concept of the holy trinity that comes to me in meditation and study is totally different from the "Father, Son, and Holy Spirit" I was taught in catechism. If I had to make an analogy, I would say that "Father" is *Spirit,* "Son" is the *body,* and "Holy Spirit" is the *soul.* ("Mother" and "Daughter" could easily be substituted for "Father" and "Son," but the patriarchal language is what most of us are familiar with due to centuries of tradition.)

I'd like to start off the book by exploring the connection between body, soul, and Spirit.

The Body: Spirit as Soul

The body is the part of us that grows from an embryo and becomes a machine composed of cells, organs, and muscles. It is what we wash and dress and feed and sustain. Just like a car, the better you maintain it, the longer (hopefully) it will serve you and remain efficient.

Sometime between conception and birth, Spirit enters the body as a soul. The soul is Spirit incarnate. Don't think of yourself as a body that has a soul, but rather as Spirit that needs a body. Spirit permeates *everything*, and in me—in this body I call James Van Praagh—it is my soul.

While on Earth, I am Spirit that requires physical form in this dimension so I can experience conditions and learn lessons that other realms don't provide. I enjoy food, art, literature, music, and other things that speak to or feed my soul. My soul experiences love, hate, betrayal, sympathy, forgiveness, empathy . . . you name it. Earth is a schoolroom, and the soul is the student.

The Soul: Our Eternal, Interdimensional Self

My soul is unique to me, but at the same time, it is a part of the whole and connected to everything. That connection is filtered through our physical senses, so it may not seem like it is always there. The emotion that we call love enables us to feel this connection, and extraordinary circumstances (such as the events of September 11) can certainly make us feel it as well. We are all the same energy, but Earth provides us with so many different physical guises that sometimes it's difficult to acknowledge that truth.

We often hear people say, "I am God," and it's true: our souls are Spirit, God, Allah, the Divine—whatever you choose to call it—on Earth. Our bodies are limited by the constraints of the physical dimension, but our souls are outside of linear space and time and transcend our physical selves.

The soul is the unique core of our self and the consciousness of who we are. It has crossed many oceans of lifetimes, experiences, and expressions of being. It's filled with infinite creative possibilities to manifest itself, and it's distinct in its own development and expression. The mediumistic term I choose to use when I'm communicating with a discarnate being is *soul-to-soul communication.*

I was once discussing the idea of the soul with my good friend Debbie Ford, the great life coach and developer of The Shadow Process. She described the soul as that part of us that never dies; it carries all the messages and lessons of the past and will carry all the messages and lessons into the future. I loved that. I told her that in my work, once a soul returns home to the Spirit World, it is the *soul* and not Spirit that I am able to communicate with. This is a very important distinction.

(Not long after that conversation, my dear Debbie made the transition, but I am still able to receive messages from her. Although she was emotionally conflicted about leaving her son, other family members, and friends in the physical, the first thing she said to me about her transition was "Oh my! It was so easy!")

The Spiritual Realms

The soul carries within it all the memories of our physical experiences through eons of time and existence. But when we transit into the Spiritual Realms, our consciousness is opened to not only the enormous wholeness of our own particular soul, but the vast awareness of Spirit.

I love the Bible verse of John 14:2: "In my Father's house are many mansions . . ." I believe this to mean the different planes within the Spiritual Realms that our souls are drawn to (after the death of the human body) based upon our earthly thoughts and words and deeds. These include the *Astral Planes,* the *Mental Planes,* and the *Celestial Planes.*

— Your personality, memory, and mind are all contained in your astral body. When your physical body dies, the "real you" is still in your astral body, and it becomes aware of life outside the human body in the **Astral Plane** to which your earthly acts have drawn you.

- The *lowest* Astral Plane draws the least evolved souls—those who have not learned the lessons of love and respect.

- The *intermediate* Astral Plane draws in those who need rest and rehabilitation after a long physical disease, traumatic experiences, or inflexible beliefs.

- The *highest* Astral Plane is what we humans would call heaven—a place of opportunity for souls to grow in spiritual consciousness.

— The soul will eventually decide whether to return to the Earth plane for more experience or to venture on to the **Mental Plane.** This level offers unlimited development of the individual soul. There is access to the accumulated wisdom of the ages.

— The highest realm is the **Celestial Plane.** Here is where the individual soul becomes one with all universal life. Christ, Buddha, and other great spiritual leaders are here.

I wish I could articulate what Debbie and countless other souls have shared with me about the realms of Spirit (which is our natural state and our true home). But I have only a human brain while on Earth, and it can comprehend only this dimension. Human words can't describe the love and peace we feel after we've "shuffled off this mortal coil."

Being a combination of our mental, emotional, and physical bodies, the soul not only is made up of all our earthly memories, but comprises the entire scope of who and what we are—not just what we perceive as "life" in the physical dimension, but our eternal, interdimensional being. When the soul rejoins Spirit, it becomes very aware of how it lived in the most recent lifetime and the impact that it had on other souls. The soul is also the repository of wisdom, love, and experiences gleaned from lifetime to lifetime. Everything we have ever experienced is kept in the soul memory.

The Spirit: The Divine Spark

Spirit comes from the Latin word *spiritus,* meaning "breath." When I think of Spirit, I think of the essence, the energy, the Divine spark, that animates and ignites our souls. Our Spirit is the highest form or aspect of who we are and is devoid of any human personality or character. It is the oneness of all things. You've heard the term *breath of God* (which means "Spirit"), and it is that which animates our souls and, in turn, lets them express themselves in the physical body.

There is only *one* Source energy, and that is Spirit. Many call it God, but that word has a religious tone that turns some people off. Religious history has transformed Spirit into an old, bearded man who judges and blesses according to whim—but nothing could be further from the truth. In catechism, I remember being told by the nuns that God is everywhere. Of course, I now know that to be true, but as a young child, I could think only of an old man watching over my shoulder and judging. (Not fun.)

I now realize that I'm God, my dog is God, every plant in my garden is God, every insect in my garden is God, and the air I breathe is God. The word *God* has been burdened with the religious connotation of an omnipotent being that is separate from and greater than us. I don't believe that. I've been making an effort to use the word *One* now instead when I am speaking about God. It's an acronym that I created that stands for "Omnipresent Nurturing Energy." When someone says "I believe in God" or "God is dead," the conversation then has to go to the semantics or definition of what the person thinks God is. To me, God is an energy and I am made of it. I am not separate from God, and neither is anything you see.

Atheism is the rejection of the belief in deities. I don't believe in deities, but I wouldn't label myself an atheist. I believe in a loving energy that permeates and animates everything. People who believe in that energy and people who believe in the Old Testament God use the same word, and that's where we run into confusion and conflict.

Choices and Lessons

As our souls are stimulated by Spirit, or the One, it expresses itself through the physical body. This expression is seen by the choices we make in our lives.

As we look around our world, we can see the myriad choices and expressions various souls can decide on. No two souls are alike; but at the core, they are the same. All souls have had different life experiences, and in a way, those experiences shape our outlook on life and the various ways to live it. Souls can express themselves through a life of compassion, tolerance, judgment, or violence.

Again, this physical world is our schoolroom—a place for the soul to live out and learn from "human" experiences—and as we live them out, these curricula mold us accordingly. When the soul has finished learning its lessons, it returns back home to Spirit, and as the soul leaves this physical dimension, the Spirit energy remains fully intact.

I often think of Glinda, the Good Witch from *The Wizard of Oz*, when I contemplate the soul returning to Spirit. Remember the image of Glinda inside her bubble, traveling up, up, and away? Think of Glinda as your soul and Spirit as the bubble as you make the journey home. The soul returns to Spirit, and just as the body is an expression of the soul, so too is the soul an expression of Spirit.

The Meaning of Spirituality

I'm often asked if the work I do has opened me up to my own sense of spirituality. Of course it has. There is no way I could be personally involved with this type of work and not receive the essence of love as souls come back and share memories that they have lived with their loved ones.

At the same time, it is important to note that just because someone claims to be a medium or psychic, it doesn't necessarily mean he or she is *spiritual*. The medium may deliver facts and evidence from the deceased, but unless that person is attentive to the spiritual energy coming through, the recipient isn't getting the "wholeness" of the message. The recipient is left with a half-baked reading, and unfortunately, the intent and wholeness of the communication is absent. What a shame for the spirit, who wanted to make sure that loved ones received not only evidence but the full emotional message (which is sometimes more important than the evidential proof that consciousness survives the death of the brain).

How do people know when they are living their own spirituality? They need to be aware that they're aligning themselves with a power that is much bigger than their personality but at the same time bringing a strong sense of their self and their place in the scheme of things. Do they have a sense of "mindfulness" that goes beyond their personality and nurtures a strong sense of self?

My husband, Brian, is a great barometer for this. Even though he is not a professional in the spiritual community, he has a good sense of whether someone who is a "spiritual teacher" walks his or her talk. If a "professional" stands in front of hundreds of people at an event and speaks about mindfulness, but later when we all have dinner together, that person is rude to the waitress, Brian checks out. He has no tolerance for people who don't practice what they preach.

Awakening to Spirit

Part of my lifework is not only to demonstrate that there is no such thing as "death" but also to assist others in waking up to their spiritual side. When people live lives of spiritual awareness and mindfulness, everything they do and say can change the lives of others. Those random acts of kindness can alter someone's attitude. On a larger scale, the spiritual awareness of teachers I admire—like Doreen Virtue, Oprah Winfrey, and Deepak Chopra—can change millions.

When we are touched by Spirit in a big way, I've heard this referred to as a "peak event." Such an experience is often described as a transcendent moment of remembering; the veil has been lifted and a nugget of truth enters our consciousness. A new piece of information fits into place and seems *right*. Oprah calls these "Aha! moments."

These experiences are events that open your soul up to your spiritual heritage and remind you of who you truly are. When you're filled with Spirit, you feel a connectedness and oneness with everyone. Your soul will have a sense of joy and peace, with a focus on service to others.

Inspire = In Spirit

I love the word *inspire*. I often tell my students that to be inspired is a true gift, and I share exercises to help them to tune in to their own inspiration. *Inspire* means "in Spirit," so when people are connected to this great energy, they're creative and limitless. They're attuned to Spirit via the soul. Countless innovators, inventors, entrepreneurs, and CEOs use meditation to tap into the infinite wisdom of the Source.

Spirituality assists you in making sense of the world and who you are. It connects you with the profoundly powerful and Divine force of the Universe. No matter what life's work you're involved in, if you are inspired, you're on the right soul path. If you're looking for worldly success, abundance, inner peace, or enlightenment, no knowledge can propel you to achieve your goals as much as spiritual knowledge. My hope is that this book will inspire you to seek spiritual knowledge within yourself. You can be a well-read spiritual scholar, but unless you apply the concepts of love, compassion, and empathy to your daily life, all that book learning is for naught.

In *Unfinished Business,* I talk about how I am drawn to the story of Helen Keller. I see her life as a metaphor for spiritual awakening. As an infant, Helen became blind and deaf, and spent the rest of her life in darkness and silence. Her teacher, Annie Sullivan, was summoned by Helen's parents to try to break through that formidable barrier. Annie would finger-spell to Helen and try to make the child understand that what she was spelling meant a particular thing, like "doll" or "cake." When Helen finally makes the connection at the water pump as Annie spells "w-a-t-e-r," it truly is an inspirational moment. If you haven't seen *The Miracle Worker* with Anne Bancroft and Patty Duke, I urge you to do so.

At the end of the movie, Annie finger-spells into Helen's hand, "I love Helen." The first time I watched this scene, I thought, *Yikes! Making the connection between a physical object and a hand sign is one thing, but what about intangible concepts, like love?* If Helen couldn't physically touch love, how in the world was she to be able not only to make the connection, but to *live* it?

Of course, Helen rose to the occasion and became one of my favorite enlightened teachers, but the progression from a child ensconced in darkness and silence who ate off people's plates for sustenance to an inspirational icon and wonderful spiritual philosopher is a great metaphor for the evolution of all human souls. It was a life filled with peak events.

Religion vs. Spirituality

Many people ask me about the difference between being religious and being spiritual. I think that difference is significant. Religion is a man-made, organized belief system consisting of various creeds, teachings, rituals, and documents and usually (but not always) revolves around a deity of some kind. If people follow a specific belief system, it is their conviction that this is how they will receive a greater position on the other side.

In contrast, spirituality is the very personal search to find the greater meaning in life and one's existence in *this* world. It doesn't have to involve rituals or written words and may encompass having a love for a Divine Source, or God, and learning to use this all-encompassing energy in every situation. In being spiritual, you have a respect and love for self and an understanding of your connection to others.

There are many paths to reach the place where you treat yourself and others with kindness and feel at peace. I know many self-identified atheists who are kinder people than some spiritual or religious people, and vice versa. It's all about constructing a belief system that works for you, makes you the best person you can possibly be, and encourages you to treat others with honor. There is not one correct way. I often say that all religions have bits of the truth, but no one religion has *all* of the truth. If the holy texts of the world's religions are not viewed through the lens of love and acceptance, it does the authors a great disservice.

The one element of religion I don't like (and this is a general statement) is that some people believe that their way is the only way. Unfortunately, many of the world's wars are based upon a sense that a certain belief system is the only true word of God. It sets up a sense of "us against them."

Where religion talks a lot about God, the idea of spirituality is to practice the higher ideals that we associate with God *in our daily life*. Spirituality is a very personal journey, but the destination is always the same: *love*. The mass exodus from organized religion in the past few decades points to the desire people have to ask questions instead of being told answers, to doubt dogma without risk of condemnation, and to feel free to be themselves without judgment.

Our planet furnishes Spirit with such a diverse mix of human stories that it's a shame some people want everyone to be just like them. The human desire to judge is strong, but if we all understood that each of us has our own unique path, wouldn't Earth be a much better place?

CHAPTER TWO

CONSCIOUSNESS, ENERGY, AND THE POWER OF THOUGHT

Just as Helen Keller surely struggled to define the things she couldn't physically touch, so do we humans struggle with the concept of consciousness. A debate rages to this day over whether consciousness is a product of the brain or if the brain is merely a receiver for consciousness that already exists. When a brain dies, does that consciousness cease to exist? Or does its energy continue on even after the brain is no longer functioning? One side of the debate wants proof and tests, while the other side just accepts that energy doesn't die.

Well, it's no surprise what I (as a medium) believe, since the consciousness is what I tap into long after the brain is no longer alive. There's no debate for me since I can't deny what I actually experience.

An easy analogy is a ham radio. It's a complex machine of wires, but it's simply a box with no purpose unless there are radio waves. After the ham radio ceases to work (or "dies"), the radio waves are still there. Everything that the ham radio has ever received or sent out is still out there as energy.

The Mystery of Consciousness

Let's back up and try out a working definition: *Consciousness* is the awareness of "being." It's the sense of being a part of all there is. This sense of being changes from moment to moment. Therefore, there are many levels of consciousness. As you're reading this book, you're conscious of the feel of the pages, of scanning and absorbing the words, of the sounds and smells in your environment, and perhaps of one or two random thoughts passing through your mind. This is your consciousness or awareness at this moment. It flows easily from one moment to the next, and the awareness is obviously external or internal.

Throughout recorded history, humans have sought to define consciousness, and of course, there are many theories and beliefs as to what it actually is. I don't happen to think that the reality of consciousness is a knowable thing while we're down here on Earth using our physical brains. We certainly can get glimmers or pieces of the puzzle, and it's enthralling to share ideas and hypotheses, but after all is said and done, the concept is not definable. It's much too big for us humans to comprehend.

Raising Our Consciousness

That certainly doesn't mean that tools to help us elevate our consciousness don't exist. One trick I use is drawing a picture of a skyscraper and taping it on my bathroom mirror. I then label the different floors with emotions that I resonate with. For instance, my bottom floor is marked FEAR, and as the building rises, I have GUILT, PITY, ACCEPTANCE, SERVICE, JOY, PEACE, and LOVE.

Every morning as I brush my teeth or shave, I assess what my day might hold, and I find what floor I'm on. And then I make a concerted effort to advance to the next-highest floor. I try to live that day at that level. Let's say that I've just read a rude comment on my Facebook page or YouTube channel. I might be feeling *pity* that I'm misunderstood. I consciously decide to *accept* that I am on this planet to *serve,* because that brings me *joy.* I have already made myself feel better in the time it takes me to brush my teeth.

I also use the image of my skyscraper when I meditate. Much as people can sit in silence and lower their blood pressure (as studies in meditation have shown), I visualize my skyscraper and try to *elevate* my consciousness.

As a start, see what levels your thoughts and behaviors seem to fall into. It is a rare person indeed who can consistently remain in the upper levels, and you should never judge yourself against others. The goal is to raise your own consciousness, not make it a competition. Everyone's levels will fluctuate according to what's going on in their lives. I also use this visualization to help me better understand what drives people and why they make specific choices.

Most important, what can we *do* to raise our consciousness to a higher level? Remember that everything around us can affect our level of consciousness: the books we read, the music we listen to, the television shows we watch, the company we keep, and what we do in our spare time.

Try drawing a skyscraper of your own, and make the emotions personal to you. Imagine what the world would be like if every person, every morning, made a conscious effort to push the "up" button of the elevator of their skyscraper.

Energy Never Dies

When I first started doing spiritual work about 30 years ago, I always discussed the concept of energy with my clients. I would tell them that everything is energy, and it's always in constant motion: the molecules in dense things move slowly; in lighter things they move faster.

When I used to broach the subject of energy decades ago, people would look at me like I was speaking a foreign language. Nowadays, the subject of energy has gone mainstream:

- "I like you! You've got good energy!"
- "The Realtor showed me a house with bad feng shui."
- "Send me some positive energy during my interview."
- "Your boyfriend has a creepy vibe."
- "The good energy you give out, you'll get back."
- "You thought so, too? We must be on the same wavelength!"

The theories about energy change as quickly as technology. The professionals can't keep up, much less the average Joe. I'm certainly no scientist, so all I can tell you is what I believe: energy never dies, but it can change form. I also believe that quantum mechanics and spirituality will eventually meet and that what we've all been saying about "God is everywhere" will be validated. We're just putting it in lay terms.

Quantum Energy:
Science Meets Spirituality

Quantum mechanics has fascinating things to say about energy: for example, that subatomic particles can be in multiple places at the same time and don't follow just one path. And since everything we perceive as "real" is made of atoms, the same laws would apply to what we call the material world. The Divine Force, or God, actually exists, and it certainly isn't a judgmental, old bearded man sitting on a throne in the clouds. It's a benign energy that permeates everything and everyone.

Energy is a concept that's been around since recorded time. Ancient civilizations such as the Egyptians used it for healing; pick up any book about the pharaohs and you'll notice that they're gripping cylinder-like objects. These cylinders (one made of copper and the other of zinc) were harmonizers of the two basic flows of human energy, which they called *Ba* and *Ka,* corresponding to the Yin and Yang of Eastern tradition. The Chinese mapped specific energy meridians in the body to strengthen and heal. We commonly know this as acupuncture. Many native traditions and shamans recognize the relationship between energy and the body in the context of healing.

Modern science doesn't yet have a way to reliably detect this energy, but brilliant minds, like Amit Goswami, Ph.D., are on the leading edge of the science/consciousness confluence. Dr. Goswami has been called the father of modern quantum theory and is a leading figure in the scientific community who believes in the existence of a spiritual dimension. If you haven't seen the documentary *The Quantum Activist,* I highly recommend it. It is the story of Dr. Goswami's journey into the spiritual to explain the seemingly inexplicable findings of quantum experiments.

I personally find that the trouble that science and spirituality have in reaching common ground is one of semantics. When one person says the word *God,* another person may automatically tune out, thinking that it is the Old Testament God. It would be great if we could agree on a word that means the "energy of everything," a benevolent force that doesn't have the connotations of an overseer or a deity.

Dr. Goswami defines God as "consciousness in its creative aspect." That's a lovely definition, but I'm still waiting for the terms that science and the layperson can bring to the table and make each other understood. There are extremists on both sides rattling their swords, and the rest of us in the middle continue to wonder what all the fuss is about.

Perceiving Energy

My senses are very open to perceiving energy. As a psychic, I know whether I can trust someone from the moment I meet him or her. Friends ask me to go house hunting with them because I will know if the home is right for them. As a medium, I must raise my slow Earth vibration higher so that I can communicate with disincarnate beings, whose vibration is very fast. They must slow their vibration down, and we meet in the middle. ("Medium"—get it?)

If I've said it once, I've said it a thousand times: everyone is psychic to a certain degree. We're all able to perceive energy in the form of premonitions, "gut feelings," and intuition. It just takes practice to develop it. (Meditation is the first step, and I've written some guided meditations for you that are at the back of the book.)

The energy I use and tap into in order to do my psychic work is exactly the same as yours. I've just had more experience discerning it.

A question I'm asked a lot at my seminars concerns the difference between the "Source" energy and "Spirit" energy. I tell them it's the same, but when it's in physical form, we commonly refer to it as the soul. An analogy I use is the following: Envision the "Source" energy (also called Cosmic, God, and Divine energy) as a vast unending ocean. If some of that water is poured into a vessel or vase (or human), it's still the same water, but it is more confined and limited. When the human body dies, the water is returned to the vast ocean from whence it came.

The Power of Thought

All energy can change its character based on our thoughts. Thoughts affect and alter energy. Everything we see first originated as a thought—the great painter of the world. As a medium, I've intuited many times that all physical matter on Earth derives from a higher mental level. Each work of art, each invention, every new medical breakthrough . . . was first created in the Spiritual Realms and eventually trickled down to a recipient as "inspiration" or "droplets of God."

Clients frequently say to me, "Tell my mom I love her!" and I reply, "You can tell her. She hears you." Souls are very alive in "heaven" or in the Spirit World. They live in a dimension that is all thought. They can communicate with each other and oftentimes with their loved ones who are still in the physical.

We humans often say things to each other like "I thought of my dad today." We think we are the originator of the thought. Did you ever consider that perhaps it's your loved one impressing a thought into your consciousness to let you know that he or she is around? Your loved ones who have made the transition can hear your thoughts loud and clear. They often describe the thought as brilliantly colored if it's a loving one, but if it's a fear-based thought, it is seen as dark and dull. This is why whenever I teach a class, the first thing I advise the students to do is take responsibility for the thoughts that they create, because thoughts are real and can have a profound impact on every aspect of their lives.

It's difficult for us humans to lend credence to the idea that a "thought" is a real thing, because we are unable to see it. But we know that there are many "waves" darting through the air such as sound waves, microwaves, and radio waves. We take for granted that they exist even though we don't see them.

When you consider your thoughts, know that they are as real to the subconscious of the person you're thinking about as if you picked up your cell phone and said them out loud. Take responsibility for your thoughts; they're not just yours. They go shooting out of you to the intended target just like arrows. That's why meditation is so relaxing—your archers can take a break!

Thoughts are creative energy, and they carve, create, and forge your future destiny. Right now as you read and absorb these words, the experience you're living is a sum total of all the thoughts you've ever had. This is the reality you've created for yourself based upon your thoughts. Some of these you remember, and some you don't. But it's not possible to think one thing and live another. If you want harmony in your life, you must have harmony in your thoughts.

Energy + Emotion

The major fuel that gives a thought focus and energy is emotion. Every time I communicate with the Spirit dimension, it is with thought. But the most incredible messages I am able to receive are the ones that are accompanied with strong emotion. When I demonstrate spirit communication at large events, I don't pick people out of the crowd. My guides are with me, communicating with the departed loved ones who want to make contact, and my guides gravitate to those souls who express emotion.

Everyone has spirit guides, and they can change with our earthly circumstances. We have:

- **Personal guides,** who are people we've known in the physical dimension
- **Mastery guides,** who are drawn to us based on certain activities we're currently engaged in

- **Master teachers,** who are very evolved and
  may never have incarnated on this physical
  plane

The guides who are usually with me during my mediumship work are Harry Aldrich, who was a doctor in London in the 1930s, and Chang, who is my master teacher and hasn't incarnated for many decades. My mother, Regina, who passed from the physical in the 1980s, also assists me.

If a thought like *My daughter is in the audience . . . I died when I fell off a ladder* comes into my mind during a reading, it doesn't resonate with me as much as the thought *My daughter is in the audience . . . I was never able to tell her I love her in life, but I want to now.* The thought suddenly becomes alive, and it's easier for me to pick up the wholeness of the emotional message.

The stronger the emotion you put into a thought, the more life and creativity you are giving it. If you add motivation and intent behind the emotional thought, you're adding an extra boost of fuel, making it more direct and focused. Now, once you get the hang of that, throw in the best ingredient of all: *love.*

Love is actually Spirit energy—it permeates everything—but here in the physical dimension, we don't always access that energy. The objective of this book is to help you realize that manifesting the energy of love is your most important assignment on Earth. So if you back your thought with love, there's no stopping it!

A very good habit to get into when you wake up in the morning is to create an intention and send that thought out with love. If you get into this routine, I guarantee that your life will change. (I include some affirmations and meditations in this book that you can use for this purpose.)

The last thing I want to share with you in this chapter is to keep your thoughts focused on what you have instead of what you don't have. If you send the message out to the Universe that there is lack, the Universe will make sure that lack is amplified. Whatever your focus is, the Universe will provide. God says "yes"; the ego says "no." Think positively, because positive thinking is more in alignment with your soul. Negative thinking will bring confusion and bitterness. Remind yourself several times a day to bring your mind to a positive place and send that positivity out.

CHAPTER THREE

NEAR-DEATH EXPERIENCES, OUT-OF-BODY EXPERIENCES, ASTRAL PROJECTION, AND REMOTE VIEWING

Every one of us has an innate curiosity about *who* and *what* we are. We wonder why we're on this planet and where we come from. We also share a desire to understand where we go after we die. If we accept the law of physics that says energy cannot be destroyed, where does ours *go?* And does the energy that departs our bodies retain memories and emotions? Does our personal consciousness survive without a body and brain?

These are all very heady questions that have pre-occupied humans since the dawn of time. The rational person would say, "I guess I won't really know until I die." And up until recently, we haven't had a whole lot of testimony from people who have died and come back to tell us about it. I'm sure the near-death experience has happened to countless people throughout history, but it hasn't been until past few years that they've felt comfortable relating their experiences, for fear of being called delusional, crazy, or liars. Even while writing her groundbreaking work on bereavement called *On Death and Dying,* published in 1969, Elisabeth Kübler-Ross was dissuaded from including a chapter on patients who had "died" and returned to tell of it, because her publisher was afraid she would become a laughingstock. Against her better judgment, she left out all that information she had garnered, because she didn't want her bereavement work to suffer from what many considered quackery.

We all have a sense sometimes that our souls exist outside space and time as we know it. But there are millions of people whose souls have left the boundaries of the physical world and have come back to share with us their experiences in a dimension much bigger, more intricate, more beautiful, and more loving than we could ever fathom. I've often thought it would be like returning from a trip to Tahiti and trying to explain your experience to your cat!

Near-Death Experiences

Near-death experience, or NDE, is a term coined by Raymond Moody in his great book *Life After Life.* NDEs are experiencing a surge in the media right now as more and more people seem accepting of the concept. Not only are there popular books by regular folks like Betty Eadie and my friend Dannion Brinkley, but several prominent physicians and scientists have also written hugely successful books on the topic. One is *Evidence of the Afterlife: The Science of Near-Death Experiences,* by Jeffrey Long, M.D. (with Paul Perry), and another is *Proof of Heaven: A Neurosurgeon's Journey into the Afterlife,* by Eben Alexander, M.D.

Dr. Alexander is an American neurosurgeon who fell into a coma caused by *E. coli* bacterial meningitis. While unconscious with his neocortex basically offline, Dr. Alexander had a variation of the typical NDE—and what I mean by a "typical" NDE is a sense of peace and painlessness, a feeling of unconditional love, and being met by loved ones who preceded us in the death process. But what was atypical was that he was greeted by a stranger, instead of his father, who had passed recently, or another loved one he recognized. After his recovery, Dr. Alexander (who had been adopted) later discovered that the woman in his NDE was actually his biological sister, who had died some years before. He had never seen a photograph of her, but after his recovery, he recognized her instantly as his guide during the NDE.

I find Dr. Alexander's story very compelling. Of course, the skeptic community was, to put it mildly, skeptical. I have no reason to doubt the veracity of Dr. Alexander's story, but the skeptics would have you think he is lying just to make a buck on a book. First of all, I think Dr. Alexander, an established neurosurgeon, would have more to lose by coming out with his story; and second, as a neurosurgeon, he probably was not hurting for money, either. I think it was more a case of the skeptics experiencing "cognitive dissonance reduction," which is a fancy way of saying that if something doesn't fit into your established paradigm of how the world operates, then the importance of that "something" must be reduced. Meaning that if a person survives a NDE and tells the story of an afterlife, and you don't personally believe in an afterlife, then either the person has to be crazy or lying, or there is some scientific or medical explanation for it.

I have much more respect for someone who says, "I don't have an explanation for that," than someone who immediately resorts to name-calling and mean-spiritedness. I was also flabbergasted to learn that among the harshest critics of survivors of NDEs are not the skeptic or scientific community (that is to be expected), but instead are some members of the religious community who believe that only those of their own faith are accepted on the other side with love and compassion.

My NDE

Back in 2008, I had an incredible life-changing experience, a mini-NDE, if you will, which I recount in my workshops. I had been in Los Angeles attending meetings, and I stopped at a neighborhood deli for a salad. Later that night at the hotel, I was violently sick and came to the realization that I had food poisoning. I drove home immediately, which was a 90-minute drive, stopping occasionally on the shoulder of the freeway to heave.

I called Brian, who was at work, to come home and take care of me. I called my doctor, and she prescribed an anti-nausea medication and told me to stay hydrated and ride it out. The medication didn't work. Even though I wasn't eating, every hour I had to run to the bathroom to empty my stomach. I told Brian and my doctor that there was blood in my vomit. Neither of them seemed too concerned about my statement since that is not uncommon with food poisoning. I guess I should have been more specific, but in my sickened state I wasn't thinking correctly. Instead of saying, "There is blood in my vomit," I should have said, "My vomit is blood."

On my last trip to the bathroom, I passed out and fell to the floor before reaching the toilet. Blood rushed up my esophagus and out of my mouth, covering the floor. Brian later said it looked like a murder scene. Needless to say, he promptly called 911.

In the meantime, I had popped out of my body and was looking down at the scene. I had the strange sensation of being out of time. I knew that I wasn't *in* my body, but I also knew that I was not dead. As I hovered near the bathroom ceiling, my cousin Patricia (who had completed suicide 30 years before) appeared up there with me. I asked her telepathically what was going on. She comforted me and said, *"It will all be over soon."*

My first thought was *"Pat, can you be more specific? Do you mean my life will be over soon or this experience will be over soon?"*

Patricia disappeared, and I became aware of a ribbon coming out of the top of my head that was connected to a sort of tapestry. I could see that if I showed fear, the ribbon would alter the tapestry, turning it a murky color. If I felt peace, the ribbon changed color, and in turn changed the tapestry to a lighter pastel. I became aware that my tapestry was connected to a larger matrix, which I sensed everyone else was attached to by their own ribbons. I had the realization that at the time of death, we are able to look over the tapestries that we have created and see how our personal tapestry fused with and altered the larger human tapestry. (I'd never been aware of this "tapestry" before, but I've often used it in my daily meditation since then. As we pass out of the physical, I believe that we can see if we have left behind a piece of art or if we have left behind something that has made the human tapestry less beautiful.)

The tapestry disappeared, and out of the corner of my eye, I saw a garden in the distance and a lone figure picking flowers. I walked toward it, and as I approached, I recognized the figure as my father (who had transitioned a few years prior), but he appeared to be about 30 years old. He smiled at me and extended a flower and said, "It's not your time yet." The next thing I knew, I was on my bathroom floor, with Brian crying out my name.

The paramedics arrived shortly, and I was taken to the hospital, where I was diagnosed with a Mallory-Weiss tear. Basically, I had retched so much from the food poisoning that I tore the lining of my esophagus, and my stomach would continually fill up with blood that trickled down from the tear. I would throw up the blood and feel better, and then it would fill up with blood again, which would make me nauseated, and it would start all over again. I was basically bleeding out.

Seven days in the hospital and many blood transfusions later, I was able to return home. If Brian hadn't been there, I probably would have died on the bathroom floor.

Remember the skyscraper I use as a meditation to elevate my consciousness? I believe that meditation can affect the human tapestry that I saw in my NDE: the more people who are thinking positive, loving thoughts, the brighter and more vibrant their personal tapestries become, which in turn makes the overall human tapestry thrive. Everyone is responsible for their own tapestry, and the more of us who lead mindful lives, the more we stay in the upper levels of our skyscraper and the more brilliantly the tapestry shines.

Since my NDE, I have done some research, and I discovered that besides the feelings of peace and love that survivors experience, many people have observed a "weblike" matrix of interconnecting lights existing above and around humans. I think this matrix might be what is commonly referred to as the *Akashic records,* an energetic imprint of every thought, action, emotion, and experience that has ever occurred. Sometimes called the "Collective Consciousness" or "The Book of Life," it's the vibrational record of every soul and its journey. Everyone has the power and right to access the Akashic records because, as souls, we *are* the records.

The American mystic Edgar Cayce (1877–1945) was able to use his subconscious mind to tap into the Akashic records (an infinite number of other subconscious minds) and interpret them through his objective mind in order to effect healings. In other words, Cayce was able to go into a self-induced sleeplike state, tap into the wisdom of Cosmic Mind, and (even though he had no medical training whatsoever) impart remedies that helped thousands.

The majority consensus of survivors of NDEs is that they are unable to deny that their consciousness survives outside of their bodies—that we are able to be fully aware and awake yet not be inside a body. It's life-changing, to say the least. People reprioritize their lives, become more loving, more positive, and more giving. People who live with someone who's had an NDE can't help but change themselves, so the benefits of an NDE become a shared experience.

The good news is that anyone can reap these benefits without having to die and come back, because an out-of-body experience is a form of NDE, and it can be accomplished with practice and training.

Out-of-Body Experiences

The term *out-of-body experience,* or OBE, was first introduced in 1943 by George N. M. Tyrrell and later recorded in his book *Apparitions,* but it was Robert Monroe who popularized the term. Monroe, a broadcaster by profession, became interested in the effects of sound patterns on consciousness in 1956, and he became a pioneer in the field of "learning" during sleep. (If you were like me as a young adult, you probably had several cassettes—with subjects like abundance, motivation, and decreasing bad habits—by your bedside that you would pop into the tape player as you went to bed. That was one of the legacies of Robert Monroe.)

Monroe became one of his own test subjects, and during his investigation, he began to experience a state of consciousness *separate* and apart from his body. These spontaneous occurrences significantly changed the focus of his research. He described this state as an "out-of-body experience," and a new field in the study of consciousness was born. In 1971, he published *Journeys Out of the Body,* which to this day remains the "bible" of OBEs. He continued to study and research this phenomenon, and he later opened a center in Virginia called The Monroe Institute. Tens of thousands of students have attended The Monroe Institute, for various reasons: to create purpose and meaning in life, to explore consciousness outside of space and time, to tap into personal healing potentials, and much more.

One of the classes taught at the institute that intrigues me is called "Lifeline." I first learned of it while watching a TV show on the Bio channel called *The uneXplained*. Human subjects are taught to not only travel outside of their physical bodies but also guide disincarnates that have exited physical existence and have not made the complete transition to the astral dimension. The theory works on the premise that some lost souls vibrate at such a slow rate that they're not able to "see" spirit helpers (who are vibrating much faster) who are there to chaperone them. It takes a human, having an OBE at a slower vibration, to help guide the trapped spirit to the light. It is also called soul rescue.

There are many people who have spontaneous OBEs, but they can train and learn to control them. Most people can develop the ability to initiate an OBE, and many become aware of an increase in other psychic abilities. The benefits of practicing OBEs are as myriad as the students themselves. They include:

- A profound sense of "knowing" versus "believing"
- Obtaining personal answers
- Decreasing the fear of death
- Experiencing past lives
- Encountering disincarnate beings and guides

There are various ways to initiate an OBE, but the most common involve a relaxed state between consciousness and sleep and intent to leave the physical body. *Intent* is the key word here, since you may have the intent to meditate for a particular reason and/or the intent to leave the body for a particular reason.

Astral Projection

As I understand it, an OBE is a generic term for anytime the consciousness leaves the physical body. *Astral projection* is a form of OBE, but with travel to other dimensions as the distinguishing feature. If you're looking at your body from the ceiling of your bedroom, that would be an OBE, but if you traveled to higher realms, that would be astral projection. The intent of your OBE would be to travel into the dimensions closest to Earth known as the Astral Planes, said to be the first level the soul will go to upon death of the physical body or during an NDE. When a soul enters it, the colors, sounds, and emotions are so unlike what we experience on Earth that survivors of NDEs have no words to describe it.

Practitioners who astral-project are connected to their physical bodies by what is known as the "silver cord," much like the tether for an astronaut who is space walking or an umbilical cord. During an NDE, you are tied to the physical body, but if the cord is broken, there is no returning. You should have no fear of the silver cord breaking during a conscious OBE or astral projection. It is only during an NDE that the connection can be broken if the human body is released.

At night during our sleep state, our astral body (connected by the silver cord) can travel the Astral Planes spontaneously. We can visit our loved ones who have made the transition, and we can seek counsel from our guides and teachers. This is where the phrase "Let me sleep on it" becomes clear.

If we're having a difficult time with an earthly problem, how does sleep help us come to a proper decision? Through the advice we get from astral beings, of course. In the morning when we wake up, the conscious mind doesn't recall the visits, but the advice that was given to our subconscious seems to make the decision much easier. Sometimes we will recall having interactions with our departed loved ones, which can also have a very calming effect.

In order to consciously astral-project, we must have awareness or a sense that there is a place beyond this three-dimensional world (which we experience with our human bodies/shells) that we're able to visit with our astral bodies. The astral body is an exact replica of the human body, but the energy isn't dense and we're able to travel to other dimensions with our consciousness intact. To become adept at astral projection can take a lot of practice. Meditation, relaxation, intention, and absence of fear are key.

Many people have asked me if drugs, such as LSD, can elicit an OBE. I have never tried LSD, so it's not a recommendation I am comfortable making. I did, however, have an experience with *ayahuasca,* which is a brew made from the combination of leaves of a particular plant and a vine (which contains a substance that allows ayahuasca to be efficacious when taken orally) found in the Amazon rain forest. It was a ceremonial setting, and I was there with several experienced shamans, so I felt comfortable. I was leading a spiritual excursion through Brazil (which is a country I love), and we were invited by the leaders of a religion called Santo Daime to attend a ceremony where ayahuasca, or Grandmother Medicine, would be used.

I purposely left the group for a day to experience the ceremony alone before I could recommend it to anyone. Lasting eight hours, it involved not only the ceremonial drinking of the tea but also drumming and chanting. The leaders, knowing that I was a famous medium from the United States, had invited several Brazilian mediums to sit with us. I had a very profound and insightful experience, but afterward, I knew that I could recommend it only to a few of the participants who had traveled with me. It's not for everyone; there is a lot of purging that takes place—physically and emotionally.

When I returned to the States, I did research on ayahuasca and discovered that it contains dimethyltryptamine, or DMT, which is naturally produced in the pineal gland. But if ingested in controlled amounts, it can produce conscious travel outside of the body. There is a fascinating book called *DMT: The Spirit Molecule,* by Rick Strassman (as well as a documentary by the same name), and the super-inquisitive TV host/comedian Joe

Rogan talks about DMT on his always entertaining podcast, *The Joe Rogan Experience.* A British writer named Graham Hancock gave a TEDx talk about consciousness and his experience with ayahuasca, and there was a huge brouhaha when the TED team pulled the video from YouTube. One side cried censorship, while the other called the talk pseudoscience—and the debate rages on.

DMT is an illegal substance in most of the world, and for someone who is interested in astral projection, I would recommend contacting The Monroe Institute's website instead of seeking out a psychedelic.

Remote Viewing

The Monroe Institute also has a remote-viewing program. Remote viewing allows a perceiver (the viewer) to describe or give details about a target that is inaccessible to the normal senses due to distance. Back in 2002 when I was hosting a daytime TV show called *Beyond,* I had an opportunity to meet with a remote viewer and put him to the test. We sent one of the show's producers to a secret location to act as the "target." The remote viewer went into a room for 30 minutes with some paper and a pen to draw any shapes and/or write down any descriptions or impressions that came to him. The remote viewer was only given the target's name—nothing else that would influence him.

After 30 minutes in silence, the remote viewer came back and showed the audience and me his results. He had drawn a picture of a staircase and said it was in constant motion. He wrote down that there was water, and it was also moving. Off to the left of the target, he drew a series of triangles with circles interspersed among them. He was totally correct—the producer was at a shopping mall, seated between an ornamental waterfall and a Christmas tree decorated with round ornaments, watching people on the escalator. I was duly impressed.

In the 1970s, the United States military funded a program to investigate the contribution remote viewing could add to clandestine programs. It was top secret at the time and has been recently declassified. Called the Stargate Project, it officially ceased operation in 1995 after it was declared unsuccessful. The participants in the project beg to differ, however, and say that the program was ended because of the ridicule factor. Much like the position of Dr. Kübler-Ross's publisher, the stigma of anything that smacked of parapsychology was too controversial to stand behind.

The major difference between remote viewing and an OBE is that remote viewing is a controlled shifting of awareness that is performed in a waking state of consciousness. The viewer is totally awake and responsive, with the mission to download information regarding a distant location. Half of your consciousness stays with you, and half of it goes to the target site to gather information. It's a skill, and anyone can achieve results with patience and practice.

When you start to take the time to look inside of yourself and attempt to connect with the unseen world, only then can you begin to comprehend your soul for what it truly is. The mystery of life doesn't seem so mysterious if you venture inward and listen to your soul's voice.

Our perception of reality is, unfortunately, filtered through our ego selves. We become lost and judge everything based on just five senses. When we look at the world around us, it may be our eyes that are viewing everything and our ears that are hearing everything, but it is our souls that are recording, memorizing, and cataloging each experience.

If you train your mind to assimilate these experiences with love, tolerance, and giving, you are feeding your soul the proper nutrients for its health and evolution. Learn not to feed your soul the junk food of judgment and intolerance. If you consider yourself to be "spiritual," then the tools to living a mindful life are obvious. But simply *knowing* the tools really means nothing unless you practice them. All the spiritual knowledge in the world is for naught unless you walk your talk.

PART II

THE
SOUL'S
HOME

CHAPTER FOUR

DEATH: THE DOORWAY HOME

Every day on Earth, our souls carry around a physical body whose cells are constantly growing, dying, and changing. Without these bodies, our souls couldn't spend valuable time on the physical dimension learning and evolving. A scuba diver needs the warmth of a wet suit, a tank of oxygen, a compass, and a clock to wander the depths of the ocean. So, too, do our souls need the *body* to accomplish our tasks on Earth. And just as the diver's oxygen tank eventually empties, our bodies ultimately stop functioning.

The diver doesn't spend his entire time underwater fretting about when his oxygen will run out. He knows that it will happen sooner or later, so he just enjoys marveling at the sights below the surface. He may be having a great time or just come upon an interesting shipwreck, but when the clock goes off, it's time to go to the surface. There are no two ways about it. It certainly doesn't mean that he can't go back down again later. It's just part of the experience. When the diver surfaces, he may slap on a new tank and dive back in, or he might lie on the boat and contemplate the journey he's just completed.

Throughout history, humans have looked upon death as something to fear. It's fear of the unknown. It's because God, in infinite wisdom, has awakened our awareness of reality while we're in the depths of the ocean with a finite amount of oxygen, and we don't know what will happen when the tank runs out. We don't know that above the surface is the actual reality: our real "home." We'll dive with many friends, and when their tanks run out, they'll have to go. We'll miss them, of course, but when our time is up, we'll see them topside. The last thing our friends would want is for us to spend the rest of our time mourning their absence. If we are to live with any measure of peace and die with any sense of acceptance, it is up to us to come to terms with how we view "death."

Death Is Merely <u>Change</u>

There is a monologue from Shakespeare's play *As You Like It* that begins:

> All the world's a stage,
> And all the men and women merely players:
> They have their exits and their entrances;
> And one man in his time plays many parts . . .

I am very fond of that quote, and I'd like to take the liberty of expanding on it. Before the "actors" make their entrances, they choose the parts that they will play and whom they will play them with. And after they make their exits, they still watch us from backstage and cheer us on and root for a fine performance. When it comes time for *our* exit, they will be there in the wings to greet us, and we in turn will continue to watch the play and applaud for our fellow actors, before it's time for *them* to join us backstage. Then we can all decide on the best time to make a new entrance, and in what roles.

Everything is a process, and seeing death as "change" instead of the "end" is one of the most difficult processes that we, as humans, have to embrace. And it's a change for the better—because if people truly understood death, it would be an event they'd look forward to and celebrate.

Whenever Brian and I attend a memorial service or funeral, it's hard for him to muster up sadness. Sure, he empathizes with the mourners, but he says that the emotion he's feeling for the deceased is more like jealousy. And don't get me wrong—he's not morose or suicidal; he would just rather be at *home* than in *school*. But he's totally happy to learn his lessons and be kind to the other students, yet look forward to going home at the same time.

I, too, look forward to the day when I go "home," but my assignment here on Earth is not nearly complete. I know that my mission is to change people's perceptions about death: to demonstrate that it is merely "change" and our souls live on.

In the early 1990s, I had the honor to sit with one of the best physical mediums who ever existed: Leslie Flint. Physical mediumship differs from what I do in that the physical medium is able to manipulate energy into physical manifestations such as spirit forms, temperature fluctuations, and noises. Under test conditions, Leslie was able to produce a substance called *ectoplasm,* which formed an artificial voice box in the air. Many disincarnate beings, including my mother, would use the voice box to speak. Ectoplasm has been described as a milky, gauzy substance that exudes from the orifices (usually nose, mouth, and ears) of some mediums.

During one of the séances (which were recorded and can be found online at the Leslie Flint Educational Trust), a well-known British actress named Ellen Terry made herself known. Leslie asked Ellen what death was like, and speaking through the voice box, she said:

> *To all those who may listen, there is no need to fear the crossing from your world to this. It is a great adventure. It is the great awakening into a greater world of loveliness and beauty and freedom of thought. Truly this is a spiritual world but not as Man has depicted it. Indeed, it is so, so different and so tremendously alive, so vital, so tremendously, as it were . . . so far removed from Man's conception of things that it cannot be depicted or described. One can only feel it and know it and sense it. It is so vast and so beautiful. Do not fear that passing from your world to this. For whatever condition of life you may enter, no matter how lowly it may be, it will be a reflection of your world but according to its condition and according to your condition of passing and particularly according to your*

*development or lack of it, so you will find a condition that
will apply to you and be best suited.*

The Process of Transition

Embracing a belief in "life after death" and not fear-
ing the transition is completely different from understanding the process. What is it like for the soul to go
through the death experience? The type of death the
physical body experiences will determine the particu-
lars of the transition. For instance, if the passing is fast,
like a fatal heart attack, car accident, gunshot, or aneurysm, it is over so quickly that the soul barely has time
to even be aware of the process taking place. But if the
soul lingers through a physical illness or deterioration,
the soul can go in and out of the body frequently, depending on the state of deterioration. If the body gets to
a point where it no longer serves the soul's needs, medical science has been inspired to develop remedies for
this very circumstance, and I am a firm believer that we
should never think twice about using this option.

Brian's mother suffered a heart attack in 2009, and
the paramedics were able to get her heart beating again.
But tests later showed that the length of time between
her heart stopping and then being revived was so great
that her brain had suffered irreversible harm. The family agreed to remove her from life support, and then
morphine was administered for two days to ease her
transition.

I have no doubt that the soul of Brian's mom was out of the body as soon as she fell to the floor, but the silver cord was not completely severed until the doctors humanely intervened. For some of us, unfortunately, pain is going to occur before death. But the actual process of slipping out of the body is not painful at all.

The Will to Survive

Humans are amazing, complex animals. They have such a strong desire to survive, no matter what, that when it comes time for their souls to leave the planet, they often will resist. The primal survival instinct flows in all of us; there is an inner drive to survive. We'll often put ourselves in "protective mode," thinking that we'll have control over our lives and deaths, and in reality when we try to hold on, it goes against our natural rhythm and causes resistance, which manifests itself as conflict.

When working with the dying, I have found that there are those souls who, in life, had to prove something by being in charge at all times. And at the end of their lives, if things are not in their control, they seem to hold on as tight as they can, instead of just letting go. When they think they have control, or don't think they will die, their souls will indeed motivate them and assist in their releasing. The time will come for the individual soul to open up to the awareness that it is not the body, the ego, the limitations, the thoughts, the personality, and so forth. The person is then ready to merge into the truth of his or her soul nature and realize that it is actually limitless and part of all that is. But many have a hard time letting go of what they think of as real: this body, this life. Oftentimes the soul needs to receive encouragement or permission to leave the physical.

When my father was close to passing, in 2004, he was in the hospital in a coma, and the doctors gave him about four hours to live. All of his family were there so that we could say our final words to him. One by one, we each whispered in his ear, shared our good-byes, and reassured him that it was okay to pass on into the next world. If you've had this experience, you know it is one of the most difficult things a person has to do in life. I was the last one to say good-bye, and as I was doing so, I was keenly aware that part of my father's soul was out of the body standing right above his head.

I kept on telling him that it was okay to go. I heard him say telepathically in my head, *"I am not leaving until all of you kids agree to not fight over my house!"* I was floored and turned to my siblings and told them. My brother-in-law, Jay, made a joke that we'd all have to change our phone numbers in order to fulfill Dad's wish. We laughed and established that we wouldn't fight over his house. I told him so, and within five minutes he transitioned. We summoned the doctor, and we could tell that he was shocked that Dad had passed so quickly.

A side note to this story: His whole life, my father worked hard for that house. It meant everything to him, and in a way it reflected who he was, what he stood for, and what he had been able to achieve. He was so proud he had accomplished buying it that he was psychologically tied into it, so of course it would have been an important attachment to his physical life. We ended up selling the house, and the new owner tore it down and built a new one from scratch.

I was upset by what Dad might be thinking up in heaven, like we hadn't protected his home. But then on a train in New York, I clearly heard him say to me, *"Why are you so upset? It was my house, I lived in it, I created memories there, and now I don't need it anymore. I would rather take those with me and let someone else create a new house and new memories."*

Debbie Ford

Another experience that profoundly affected my life and my work (and is the reason I wanted to write this book) concerns the transition of Debbie Ford, which I briefly mentioned earlier. I met Debbie in the early '90s at a conference in San Francisco. Her sister, Arielle, was speaking at the conference, and afterward Debbie and I sat in the corner of a restaurant and shared dinner and got acquainted. She told me her life story, including drug addiction, failed relationships, and her issues with self-worth. I told her that she needed to write a book and share her story with the world; it could help millions of people who suffered from the same situations.

The rest is history. She wrote the book *The Dark Side of the Light Chasers*, was invited on *Oprah*, and skyrocketed into the "self-help" galaxy. Later she wrote many bestsellers, was an international speaker, created foundations, and single-handedly changed the perspective on our *shadow side*.

But to me, Debbie was always just Debbie. She never forgot her friends even with the sudden fame, and people often remarked on how "real" she remained. But with the highs, come lows. Few people knew it, but Debbie had a very rare form of cancer and had been fighting it for years. The few who knew about her condition would often hear about the different types of treatments she was investigating, always hopeful something new would take hold. The hope never stopped.

In 2011, I was speaking at a conference in Manhattan, and there was a knock on my hotel-room door. I opened it and there was Debbie, looking impish and pretty, as usual. She bounded through the door and screamed out: "Hi, honey, I missed you!"

After we got caught up on how life was treating both of us, Debbie told me she had something she wanted to ask me. We sat down, and she began.

"James, if it comes to the end and I am passing over, would you help me pass?" I was flabbergasted, but it was Debbie, so I always expected the unexpected.

"Yes, of course. If I am able, I would do anything for you," I told her.

Relieved, she thanked me and abruptly changed the subject: she was beginning to write a new book that she wanted to call *Courage,* and we talked about it. After she left my hotel room, she never brought up the subject of her death again, even though we chatted on the phone routinely.

That was to be the last day that I would see Debbie physically alive. Between both of our work and travel schedules, we never were able to be in the same location at the same time again.

In early 2013, I answered a call from a mutual friend, Jorge, who phoned me late one night. His usually upbeat voice was low and serious. "I'm at Debbie's; it's not looking good. She wants to talk to you."

I was in shock with the realization that the end was here so quickly. Jorge handed the phone to Debbie, and I heard a very low, faint voice say, "James, I think it is tonight. I'm getting ready to go."

I was in shock and started to cry. I knew this was the moment she had spoken to me about in my New York hotel room, and I had to give her something. I forced out, "I love you, Debbie. I am here. If you feel lost, think of me and I will be there. I am with you. We can talk in thoughts."

She was getting weaker, and she barely managed to reply, "Really? Okay, I love you, too. Bye." Jorge took back the phone and passed it to Debbie's sister, Arielle. I told Arielle to tell Debbie to pretend that she was a feather and just fly away and to keep on giving her that image. Arielle assured me she would phone me when she had an update.

I was expecting a call within hours. I kept thinking of Debbie, but I couldn't reach her with my thoughts. I knew that she hadn't passed yet. I called up Arielle to ask what was happening. She told me that she had spent the night with her sister and had said her good-byes. Arielle remarked that everyone was just amazed that Debbie was holding on for so long. Even the hospice nurse had never seen a case where someone held so strongly while so ill. Arielle knew that was Debbie; she would go when she was good and ready! Arielle asked if I could do something to help, and I told her I would try my best.

After I hung up the phone, I left Brian and the dogs downstairs, and shut myself in the bedroom. I lay down on the bed and began to meditate. As I got deeper and deeper, I focused on Debbie and I began to see her face very clearly. She looked as if she was in her early 30s, and when I called her name, she looked right at me and smiled.

I mentally said to her, *"Debbie, what is the problem? Why don't you want to leave? There are people waiting for you."*

She quickly defended her position and yelled out, *"I'm a mother, James!"*

I told her that her son, Beau, would be fine, that he was in college, and the family would be looking after him.

She then dropped her doe eyes and said, *"Death is so strange; it's like I have been given a new set of keys to a car, but I don't know how to drive."* It was pure Debbie. Then she said something I will never forget for the rest of my life: *"For years I have been so concerned about teaching people how to live that now I don't even know how to die!"*

I smiled and knew this was very much the truth. In my consciousness, I began to see a parade of her past lives. I telepathically saw all her death scenes. She was a warrior, a commander, a chief, a priestess . . . and in all the lives she was killed for her belief systems. Since her current transition was imminent, I had the sense that Debbie was aware of these past lives as well. I could tell that she was conflicted and resistant.

I made sure that I got her attention and telepathically said to her, *"Debbie, those are past experiences. Right now all you have to do is look up and visualize a gold curtain."*

"Are you sure, James?" she asked.

I said, *"Yes, and look for your father. He is there with some friends of yours from Miami. Just go to them."*

I had a vision that reminded me of Dorothy skipping up the yellow brick road. But it wasn't Dorothy. It was beautiful, dear Debbie looking back at me one more time and smiling.

I came back fully into my own awareness, and I went downstairs, where Brian was watching TV. I told him what had happened, and we hugged and cried.

Suddenly the TV room went frigidly cold. Brian said, "Did you leave a door open upstairs?"

All I could say to Brian was "It's Debbie!"

Ever the pragmatist (and double Virgo), he went in search of an open door. He returned and said, "Everything is closed. You're right—it must have been Debbie." The coldness disappeared slowly, and with its receding came a feeling of gratitude and completeness. I could not hold back the tears and was interrupted by the phone ringing. I picked it up; it was Arielle.

"Debbie has passed." I told her that I knew, that she had just come to visit, and she was finally free.

It should have been very difficult for me to sleep that night, but somehow I fell into a deep slumber. At about 5 A.M., I was awakened as if someone hit my head with a sledgehammer. I opened my eyes and Debbie was in my consciousness, begging me to get to a computer. I ran out of my bedroom and went into my office, turned on my computer, and started to write every word Debbie gave me.

She kept saying, *I am free, James! I am so free! I cannot believe how obsessed I was about my body! What was I thinking? How crazy!* This struck me as extremely funny because anybody who knew Debbie knew that she was very concerned about her appearance, always wanting to look her best.

"Tell everyone not to be so involved in physical things," she continued. *"It makes it harder to let go at the end. Tell everyone that as a soul you are part of the 'oneness of the wholeness'!"*

I sat in my office for two hours and laughed and cried. I sent off e-mails to her family and friends, because she had asked me to share her thoughts. Debbie Ford is a great soul, and she wanted others to realize that *they* are great souls while still having the human experience and not wait until they pass over to come to this realization.

Our Loved Ones Await

I knew that Debbie's father was the first one to greet her as she made the transition. On the Spirit side of life, there is a telepathic "knowing" of your upcoming return.

My father had a dream about my mother (who had been dead for many years) before he fell ill. She was on a train, and she looked very young and beautiful. She invited my father onto the train, and he obliged. "She only asked me to go on the train. You weren't invited," he later told me as he recounted the dream.

After Brian's mother passed, his father was in his kitchen and he swore that his own mother (who had died in 1965) walked past him and beckoned for him to come outside the front door. His father passed within a year of that visitation.

Souls you recognize from the physical plane who have made the transition all have a task to perform as your time nears, from influencing your transition to creating a welcoming environment. Even deaths that we humans would term sudden or unexpected, like accidents or murders, are viewed well in advance on the Spirit side. Guides, family, and teachers are always aware and bound to the soul in its every move and will steer it in its progression to get back home.

You must know that *no soul ever transitions alone!* The spirit people take such care of you and exhibit such concern for you on your journey that they are all very prepared and excited for you to enter their world. It's the epitome of a "welcome home" party.

Deathbed Experiences

Despite what humans may think, there is absolutely no pain when death comes upon us and the spirit leaves the body. It is very natural and has often been described as the "ebbing of a tide." Many nurses, doctors, and family members recount stories of how dying patients will suddenly open their eyes, apparently feeling no pain at all, and reach out and speak to deceased loved ones. People will even describe how beautiful the "other world" is.

There are also documented cases in history of some very famous people who on their deathbeds suddenly became quite lucid and expressed what they were experiencing before they left the earth. The German poet

Schiller's last words were supposedly "Many things are growing plain and clear to my understanding." When Thomas Edison was close to passing away, in 1931, he suddenly awoke and exclaimed, "It is very beautiful over there!"

I recently read a book called *Stop Worrying! There Probably Is an Afterlife,* by Greg Taylor. It recounts in great detail many more deathbed visions throughout history, including a variation called a *Peak in Darien experience*—a deathbed vision where a dying person sees departed loved ones beckoning, but among those spirits is someone supposedly alive. Long before e-mail and cell phones, it could take days, weeks, or months to hear about the passing of a family member who did not live nearby. Greg recounts many documented cases where a deathbed vision included the spirit of a loved one whose death had not been known to the family yet. I find his research to be very convincing.

A Smooth Transition

In cases where a person has been ill or hospitalized for some time, the soul is often treated with extra care after the transition, because the mind still carries with it the assumption of illness. After the death of the physical body in a hospital, the same setting is re-created in the Spirit World so that the shift is not jarring. But in other scenarios where there is little to no loss of consciousness (such as a heart attack or an aneurysm), the soul will often feel as though it is entering a dream world, and as the soul's physical eyes close and its spiritual eyes open, it is suddenly outside the body and everything it experiences is incredibly light and joyful. All senses seem to be heightened, and its soul family escorts the new arrival into an astounding world of illumination.

Souls can clearly see the loving faces of their spirit family. Their loved ones have been patiently watching the twilight of the physical body and the sunrise of the soul body. The newly arrived soul may feel like it is floating in a daze, but cannot deny the incredible rapture it is receiving from its spirit family. Soon enough it will adapt and immerse itself in its new way of life. Any pain, suffering, or challenges that were part of its earthly experience are gone now. It is relieved and freed. The soul *knows* it is no longer on the earth, because emotions are heightened, color and sound are clearer, and thought is telepathic. Space is not limited, and time is not linear.

Many new souls will be advised by their guides to visit their funerals or memorial services as confirmation that they are indeed no longer of the physical. After a good friend of mine named Michael made the transition in the 1980s, his guide (an African priestess) appeared to me in my bedroom with Michael in tow because he wanted to hear from someone he trusted that he had indeed "died." After I telepathically told him that it was true, he accepted it and they both disappeared as quickly as they had come.

When souls return and walk among the earthly beings, they can feel the heaviness and denseness of this dimension and are shocked by the illusions of freedom and awareness that they felt as humans. They attempt to communicate with their loved ones by sending out thoughts to let them know that are fine and "alive," but those still on Earth are usually too clouded with loss and grief to pick up on them. The spirit will make feeble attempts, but they mostly go unnoticed.

Soon, souls understand that the earth is not the place for them. It is limiting and flat. In the Spirit World they move at the speed of a thought, and similarly, the only thing that will keep them from moving *is* the limitation of their thoughts.

Expectations of Heaven

Those in the Spirit World often say that the transition will be easier if people have some kind of understanding of what waits for them when they pass over, or at the very least what to expect. Brian's mother, who was a staunch Catholic, would never in a million years have had a reason to read one of my books, but because I was her son's partner, she always did. She has come to me many times since her passing and said that the information she'd gleaned from my books made her transition much easier than it was for her devout friends.

Those on the earth whose belief systems are limited or judgmental may have a more difficult time accepting their new world. They may still believe they are alive, because they still feel so solid, and just want to wake up. But moments pass, and these souls will begin to understand that they don't even have to say a word; they and everyone in this new world know each other by their thoughts and their character. On the earth, people could hide their thoughts and be very private about who they were, but it is quite the opposite now in the Spirit World.

One of the biggest transitions souls go through is that death has turned them inside out. Their consciousness, which needed to feel separate to function on Earth and which they assumed was theirs alone, is now revealed to be at one with everything—and always has been. The drop of water that was their earthly awareness has been released into an infinite ocean.

CHAPTER FIVE

THE SPIRIT WORLD

I remember that once while I was making an appearance on *The Joy Behar Show*, Joy had a difficult time with the concept that, at death, Hitler's soul and Mother Teresa's soul would go to the same place.

It's true that every soul returns to the Spirit World, but we have been so programmed by religion to think of "heaven" or "hell" that most of us find it hard to imagine that those two souls would end up somewhere together. The simple answer is yes, they go to the same place—the Spirit World. The complicated answer is no, they don't go to the same place *in* the Spirit World. If you put a drop of water into the Mediterranean Sea and a drop of water into the San Francisco Bay, those drops are both in the same place . . . yet not in same place.

While I sit here attempting to describe to you the geography and design of the Spirit World, it seems to be such an enormous task that I could dedicate an entire book just to the "cosmology." Therefore, I've decided to keep the descriptions succinct and convey the general characteristics of these worlds within worlds, with the understanding that there are infinite variations, levels, and planes that make up this extremely busy and real place. I will concentrate on what I believe to be the most important areas in order for you to have a broad understanding of its workings.

Worlds Within Worlds

Over the years there have been many theologians, psychologists, and poets who have written about the world of Spirit and where we go when our human bodies die. I have read many of these, and based on these works and my own work as a medium, I am laying out the basics of this dimension. Again, the truth about the Spirit World is just not knowable by humans with our limited brains. There are just educated theories. As with anything else, if what I say resonates with you, keep it; if it doesn't, then it's not meant for you. Buddha is quoted as saying, "Believe nothing, no matter where you read it, or who said it, no matter if I have said it, unless it agrees with your own reason and your own common sense."

The concept of infinity can be staggering. Larry King once asked me, "If everybody has a soul and there are a lot more people on Earth than there were 2,000 years ago, where do all these new souls come from?"

I was taken aback by the question, because it never occurred to me that some people might think that way. I always thought of Spirit as infinite and the number of souls on Earth as finite. You could have 10 people, then 100 people, then 1,000 people taking thimblefuls of water out of the ocean and just one person throwing thimblefuls back in, and you still wouldn't make a dent in the ocean.

The Spirit World is a place of Divine order: there are souls going out and souls coming in all the time. Most souls are ill-equipped to enter the spiritual dimensions, thinking instead that they are in some kind of dream, so as they cross over into their natural home, these new souls are escorted by energy that they recognize as their earthly loved ones. One of the first realizations on the part of a soul is the fact that it is itself a multidimensional being of energy. Some energy may vibrate at a very fast rate, like Mother Teresa, and some energy, like Hitler, may vibrate very slowly.

The love energy of each particular soul as it leaves the body vibrates at different rates, and the energy you happen to be vibrating at when the silver cord is broken will determine your place in the dimension of Spirit. The levels aren't deemed good or bad (that's not a concept in Spirit), just different. Some humans who made a conscious effort to use their free will to raise the energy of love on Earth (or who made the "tapestry" brighter) will gravitate to the corresponding level in Spirit, and those who lowered the energy will gravitate to a different level.

Just as the earth is composed of many countries, the Spirit World is composed of many levels. These "worlds within worlds" are energetic levels and not in a specific location. The Spirit World, or heaven, is not "up"; it's interdimensional. *Everything* occupies the same space, but the energy vibrates at different rates, and each level is a solid, real world to those beings in it.

The Astral World

The first location a soul enters upon returning to the Spirit World is referred to as the Astral Plane. I often refer to this level as the "receiving station" where each soul is met by family and friends from the past who have been involved with the soul's progression. Whenever I go to pick up someone at the airport, I can't help but think that the process must seem similar to the arriving soul when it is met by loved ones in the Spirit World. If only those left behind on the earth could experience the heightened excitement the newly arrived soul is experiencing, their grief wouldn't be so strong.

When the soul arrives, it is amazed by how similar the Astral World is to the earth; it's a place of form and structure, much like our own physical world, so as not to make the transition so shocking. There are homes, stately buildings, incredible gardens, lakes, cities, pets, and all sorts of sports and games available. This world duplicates in many ways our earthly existence and what we perceive from our earthly existence, only *finer*. While the earth is a physical world, the astral is more of a mental world created by thought. But that said, everything there appears solid and real.

Many have described having beautiful houses here, surrounded by gardens made in perfect proportion to the houses. The landscaping and homes all seem naturally placed, and each will also resemble the character of the person to whom it belongs. Everything seems to be beautiful and light and natural. It is everything one would think of in a heavenly world. It is also an environment where if a person had the desire to pursue an artistic endeavor while on Earth but never had the time to take lessons, here he or she is able to fulfill that wish. It's a creative place, filled with music and art. It seems like a place where all of your heart's desires are satisfied.

Like attracts like, so the beliefs you held on Earth about the hereafter are mimicked in the Astral World, for the sake of a smoother transition. For instance, if you have a very strong belief system as a born-again Christian, you will gravitate to an astral level that is the home of others of your belief system. The same could be said for nonbelievers or skeptics of life after death. They will of course live on, but they will be at a level in the Astral World made up of other nonbelievers who may not, at first, accept life past the physical world.

Recently, I had an experience that really brought this home to me. During a public event, I was delivering a message for a woman in the audience, speaking to her deceased husband, when out of the corner of my eye, I became aware of the soul of a man who I knew was this woman's deceased father. He stood in the corner, arms folded, and looked at me. When I acknowledged him telepathically, he said, *"Why would I communicate with you now? I didn't believe in this when I was alive."*

I was blown away, but then I realized that we *are* exactly what we think, and the environment we create matches the level of awareness we're at. It is a misconception to believe that all souls have an immediate expansion of consciousness once they leave the body. You are what you believe, and you will expand and grow and evolve in your own time.

Many people also have the false notion that once they get to the Spirit World, it will all be easy and they won't have to worry about the things they did or even failed to do while on Earth. This is not the case. While it is true that we're surrounded by love and acceptance always, we're also met on the other side of life by *all* of our thoughts, words, and deeds, as well as the people whom we might have wronged. There is no judgment, except of self. It is indeed the great leveler.

A friend of mine shared with me this fictional story that helps explain how what we think on Earth may not jibe with what we discover in the Astral World:

A very wealthy man passes over and meets St. Peter at the pearly gates. St. Peter escorts him in through the gates, and immediately the man is taken with the beauty and opulence of heaven. All around him are mansions glistening in color and light, and there are splendid meadows and breathtaking gardens. The man tells St. Peter, "This looks like some property that I owned. You know, I was one of the wealthiest men on Earth, and I used to have mansions like these everywhere. I had a staff of hundreds to do everything for me." St. Peter did not respond but continued to lead the man down a path of this new world.

As the path continued on, the man became insistent that St. Peter show him his new house. The man was sure it must be one of the incredible mansions he had been eyeing. "Where is my house? Where is it?" he asked. St. Peter just told him to follow him, that it wouldn't be much farther.

As they continued, the path grew narrower, and the steps became harder to see. The man also looked around him and noticed that the majestic meadows had turned yellow and there were patches of muddy dirt. The mansions were gone, and now they were surrounded by little shacks.

The man abruptly stopped St. Peter and said, "Hey, where is my house? You must have taken a wrong turn."

St. Peter smiled and said, "Just a few more steps and we will be there."

The man was quite confused and immediately thought St. Peter had mistaken him for another soul. He became angrier as he looked around to see the shacks had become little hovels. Insistent, the man reached out to St. Peter, grabbing him on the arm.

"Hey, where is my house? Let's go back that way!" shouted the exasperated man. St. Peter smiled and pointed to a pile of broken wood and cardboard in the distance.

He said to the man, "Over there, that is your house."

The man knew St. Peter had made a mistake, and told him so. "Is this some kind of joke? Don't you know who I am?" he asked.

St. Peter looked at the man and politely responded, "This is your new house. We could only build with the materials you sent us."

You create your own existence in the Astral World with what you created in your heart during your soul's sojourn in the earthly world. If you lived a life of closed-mindedness, intolerance, hate, and judgment, that's what you'll have to face in yourself when you pass into the world of Spirit. Some people might call it hell, but it's said in the Bible, "Whatsoever a man soweth, that shall he also reap." Your thoughts and words and deeds have consequences.

Part of coming back to the earth level and entering various situations and conditions here is to attempt to evolve to our higher nature of love. One way we can expand and grow is to change our consciousness in order to cultivate understanding and compassion for one another. While on the earth, souls create their vibratory rate with their attitudes, choices, thoughts, and belief systems. When a soul chooses to bring itself up to the vibration of love, and let go of limitations and judgments, it raises its energetic level. This is so much better if done while the soul still inhabits the physical body.

I did a reading once where Elvis Presley came through and a separate reading where Princess Diana came through. They had totally different life experiences, but they both expressed the same feeling: that the outpouring of prayers and affection from humans on Earth raised their souls to a level of the Astral Plane that they themselves didn't think they deserved. But it's all a matter of perception. Elvis and Diana went about their business on Earth, flaws and all, unaware of the impact their lives really had on others.

I am blessed to count actress and author Shirley MacLaine as a friend of mine, and once while we were having dinner, I asked her if she had an awareness of how much she has shifted the consciousness of the world. She said, "Hmm, not really."

I was stunned. I personally know hundreds of people whose lives have been changed by her writings. My husband, Brian, for instance, was raised Catholic but was a secret agnostic for most of his life. He had been taught only one belief system at a young age, and he instinctively knew that it wasn't true for him. So his only other option as a child was to believe nothing. It wasn't until he read Shirley's book *Out on a Limb* that a whole new way of thinking opened up to him that he had never before been presented with. The square peg of Brian's soul that had struggled to fit through the round hole of Catholicism slipped right through the new opening that Shirley had created. It was his peak event.

If Brian hadn't been on a higher level of awareness when he met me in 1994, we never would have worked as a couple, because he wouldn't have been able to accept what I do for a living. And if I didn't have Brian in my life, I wouldn't be able to travel and teach like I do. It's one big ripple effect. But Shirley doesn't know those stories; she knows her life as an entertainer, mother and grandmother, daughter, and sister. It's not in our human nature to acknowledge our personal contribution in inspiring the world. Humility can prevent us from seeing the forest for the trees.

But I digress . . . The point I want to make is that you may never have an earthly awareness of what it is that truly counts. Random acts of kindness such as a smile to a stranger carry more weight than attending church every Sunday out of obligation. You can literally change the energy field around you by keeping your thoughts high-minded, and only attract those who gravitate toward the higher vibration. Remember that like attracts like, so when you bring that energy into your life, only good things can happen—and what you reap may arise from something you had no conscious awareness of sowing.

The soul learns and evolves not only while on the physical plane, but also in the Spirit dimensions. In the Astral World there are a multitude of strata and levels. There are many souls who choose to stay amidst the Astral World for great periods of "time." I put the word *time* in quotes because linear time is just a tool of the three-dimensional. Time as we know it does not exist in the Spirit realms. Everything that has existed, exists now, or will exist is happening concurrently. (Trippy concept, I know, and I'll leave it to greater minds than my own to explain it.) But because we're spiritual beings having a physical experience on Earth, our awareness of time as past, present, and future is a necessary device.

The Ethereal World

Souls in the Astral World may reincarnate directly from there, or they may move up to the subtler dimensions known as the *Ethereal World*. In the astral levels, they are free to express themselves fully and are perfectly content with the experiences that this vast and eclectic world has to offer. The ties to the physical world are much stronger in the Astral World, and it brings much comfort. There are properties of the Ethereal World that will be felt on the astral levels, materializing in different ways. Some will manifest as pure inspirational thoughts or even receiving great works of creativity. It is as if those in the Astral World are the recipients of the droplets of God from the higher levels.

The Ethereal World—also known as the Thought Plane—vibrates at a higher rate than the Astral World. It seems to be made up of soul beings who have reached a point of purity of mind and thought, and really are connected to us through what is known as inspiration. All the great compositions of music, masterpieces of art, and scientific discoveries have their origins in the Ethereal World. It is a formless realm that is made up of pure consciousness. Thought and energy move about faster here than data in any supercomputer you can conceive of.

Within this Ethereal World, the slow-vibrating part of our individual selves meets the faster-vibrating part of our souls. It is the place where the "higher self" resides. This plane is filled with light and love and truth. It interacts with our mental selves and helps create abstract thoughts and acts as the doorway for higher levels of wisdom to come down and integrate with the lower aspects of our being.

As a medium, I don't have contact with entities of the Ethereal World. Ties to the personalities we were on Earth (and the physical loved ones we remember) are tenuous here. As a general rule, the longer a soul has been disincarnate, the more difficult it is for me to make a connection. And for a true mediumistic connection, I need someone from the physical who actually knew the soul. I can't just conjure up Abraham Lincoln for somebody who asks.

I recently read a great novel called *The Brief History of the Dead,* by Kevin Brockmeier. In it, the author references the belief of many African tribes that people can be divided into three categories: those still alive (humans), the recently departed (*sasha*), and the dead (*zamani*). When people die, they become *sasha* and remain *sasha* while there are still people alive on Earth who remember them. When the last person on Earth who remembers them dies, they go on to be the *zamani* and are then revered and recalled by name only.

I'm not saying that the wisdom of the Ethereal World cannot be accessed by humans, because it can. *Trance channeling* is a broad term to describe when a human has become a conduit for the wisdom and intelligence of these higher realms. Instead of communicating with the disincarnate consciousness of your recently departed uncle Joe, like I do, the trance channeler is a conduit for a connection to a higher being or beings who will impart wisdom and knowledge from those realms.

The Seth material, *A Course in Miracles,* and the Teachings of Abraham are examples of tapping into this infinite intelligence. The humans imparting this wisdom (such as Jane Roberts with Seth, and Esther Hicks with Abraham) may access the higher realms differently or define what it is that they do in different terms, but there is no denying that the information they tap into and share is not of their own consciousness.

People often ask me if, upon death, they can be greeted by their loved ones who are no longer in the Astral World but have either reincarnated back to the physical or moved on to the Ethereal World. The answer is yes. Putting a limitation on what a soul can do, where it can manifest, or how it can divide its consciousness is just us humans looking at things from our three-dimensional mind-set. The soul is not controlled by our perception of space or time.

The Celestial Realm

The Celestial Plane is often referred to as the "Angelic Realm." The souls who dwell on this level have achieved a particular degree of spiritual evolution and would be considered elevated beings. It is where angels and archangels; mystics and masters; and prophets whom we know as Jesus, Mohammed, and Buddha reside. The souls who exist here are involved in bringing the pure stream of exalted aspects of God's love down to the lower spheres. Many who reside here may have never even been on the earth plane, and indeed may be of celestial and/or extraterrestrial makeup. This energy of life is more of a light-energetic form of being. The auras of these beings are so full and bright that humans have conceptualized them as wings and halos. My dear friend Doreen Virtue is the leading expert on using the wisdom of angels and ascended masters for health and spiritual transformation.

The description of this sphere is one of an unobstructed life. There is no more heaviness or judgment. Those elements are foreign to this way of being. The entities on this level have no humanoid characteristics and are connected to all life and able to bring the best attributes of higher conditions of being to others. This is also known as the *bliss* level, where there is a feeling impossible to conceive of on the lower spheres. It is tangible yet beyond the imagination and has been described as "divine joy."

The closest analogy I could share would be the feeling two people experience when they're in love. Two people in love seem to merge into one being. They feel united and become one entity, which makes them feel, think, act, and love like one being. There is no separation between them. On this level, the souls will experience this sense of oneness, and there is no feeling of duality or light or dark. It is all one element, one consciousness.

To attain this level is to cultivate a pure, unselfish, all-embracing, and beneficent love. This is a love that is impartial and seeks nothing; it exists for the sake of love alone. The spontaneous outpouring of love that gives and asks for nothing back is the most marked attribute of beings in the Celestial Realm.

The energy of love is what the Universe is made of, and as we are enveloped into this natural rhythm, we are drawn toward perfection and transcendence. The beings on the Celestial Realm realize, on some level, that they are one with Spirit, and although they have reached the path to love, they are still evolving and are always willing to give help to all who ask.

CHAPTER SIX

REINCARNATION
AND THE MEMORIES
OF THE SOUL

Your soul has delved into the dimensions of many worlds, planets, star systems, lifetimes, positions, situations, and experiences in order to bring knowledge, insight, and understanding to the world of Spirit. Just as a bee goes from flower to flower to bring pollen back to the hive, so does your soul go from life to life to bring your unique experience back to the Source. The soul's adventures are always about learning, experiencing, expanding, and evolving.

People are constantly asking me, "What is my soul's purpose?" The easy answer is *to love unconditionally.* The energy that we call "love" is what the world of Spirit is made of; it's the natural rhythm of the Universe. If every soul was evolved to the point where we all loved unconditionally, we would have "heaven on Earth." But we're a long way from that, aren't we? Ego, pride, and judgment manifest themselves in racism, nationalism, sexism, and homophobia. "Us versus them" is a much more comfortable notion for us than "We are all the same."

Defining Reincarnation

Reincarnation is a tricky concept. It's another one of those things that we have difficulty wrapping our human brains around in its totality and purpose. Reincarnation is the belief system that souls choose to manifest in human form in order to develop their knowledge and wisdom. I know it's just semantics, but I prefer to say that the energy of Spirit chooses to come back in physical form as a soul. I don't like the concept of souls being individual while disincarnate. If you put a drop of water in the ocean, sure, those molecules are in there and separate—but good luck finding them.

Reincarnation has been the cornerstone of many belief systems and religions since the beginning of time. The reasons and motives behind the idea, however, can vary slightly. For instance, Buddhists believe that there is no eternal soul, spirit, or self but only a stream of consciousness that links life with life. Hindus believe that we come back in various lifetimes to alleviate karmic conditions and this karmic energy is what will come back to the physical level until all karmic obligations are burned off. Ancient Jews believed in reincarnation, or *gilgul*. This term means "cycle" and is mentioned in the Kabbalah—the mystical teachings of Judaism. For many centuries Christians also believed in the idea of reincarnation, and it wasn't until the Second Council of Constantinople in A.D. 553 that reincarnation was officially declared a heresy and mention of it was stricken from public texts. The powers that be didn't like the idea of people getting infinite chances to get it right, because then you wouldn't need the church to offer you salvation.

Previous Incarnations

In my work, I often meet people who constantly want to know "who" they were in a past life. I tell them that they are a sum total of every past-life experience they have ever had. Deep within the soul fabric are recorded the many lifetimes, people, and experiences it has ever gone through. The soul is a vast network of data and information. Through eons of time, it has learned to express itself and attempts to perfect its strengths and reduce its weaknesses. Within its memories are events, attitudes, behaviors, insights, opinions, and actions that can affect the current incarnation.

And this is information that you're able to know. But is it *important* for you to know? It depends on your motivation. If your motivation is to help overcome a fear or phobia that has no known origin in your current life, or if it's to help you understand more clearly why you react badly in certain situations, or if it's for spiritual transformation, then I'm all for it. If it's just to find out if you were Cleopatra, then I don't get the point.

Another question I get asked a lot is "How long do I spend in the Spirit realms before I decide to reincarnate?" Everything happens in Divine order, so there is no pat answer. The Spirit World is our home, and we spend most of our time in that dimension reevaluating and fulfilling our souls' duties. We also spend much of our "in-between" time studying and preparing for our next incarnation.

The ultimate goal of reincarnation is to bring the consciousness of love and understanding into our everyday existence. Just *being* a human presents many obstacles to this goal, but some of the lives we choose present more challenges than others. Sometimes we rise to the occasion and enrich the "tapestry," and sometimes we fail and make the world a darker place.

When Spirit chooses to return to Earth as a soul in a physical vessel, it does so knowing that it will go through various experiences and situations that assist it in utilizing knowledge of past incarnations and provide rich opportunities for it to evolve and learn. Everything is a progression, and a soul may try many times to perfect a skill and finally be given the opportunity to have it realized in the current lifetime.

This is very true of my ability as a medium. I know inherently that I have worked as a mystic, priest, holy man, monk, missionary, wizard, and so forth for many lifetimes in order to realize and perfect my perceptions, trust, and intuition to such a degree that I'm now able to act as an intermediary between the incarnate and the disincarnate worlds.

GPS for the Soul

All souls come back to the physical incarnation with a strong purpose and a plan. Remember, the overall goal is to bring love into all that you do, but on Earth, there is free will. Not following your soul's true desire (and instead succumbing to earthly lures that don't bring the energetic vibration up) is the biggest cosmic speed bump out there.

As humans, we are all led astray by power, bitterness, revenge, and envy (to name a few), and our innate path to goodness becomes a dark and winding road. *The Huffington Post* recently added a spiritual section to their website called "GPS for the Soul." I love that title, and it would be great if we all listened to the one we are born with. Instead of "In 500 feet, turn left," it would say, "Confrontation ahead. Use love and understanding." Instead of listening to that inner GPS when our pride or egos have been bruised, our default mechanism is to react in kind.

The anonymity of social media has become a breeding ground for people who think that they can be unkind or hurtful without taking responsibility for their actions. Think again. Our words and deeds belong to us, and there is no hiding from the consequences. There are nuggets of wisdom out there to help us on our path, such as "Turn the other cheek," "Two wrongs don't make a right," and "Take the high road," but we just see them as clichés. They are all truisms to remind us that even though others in our lives may be driving with their GPS off, we don't have to do the same.

Karma is a term that is bandied about a lot, but the essence of it is not always taken to heart. Karma is a benign energy—it's the intent behind that energy that makes it "good" or "bad." When a soul returns to Spirit, the human life that it just led is reviewed, and we learn where we made wrong turns and correct turns and U-turns. Before the next incarnation, we will pick out the best opportunities and situations available to afford the soul the greatest amount of growth potential. Unfortunately, a lot of the planning revolves around cleaning up some karmic debris that we've left behind. It's difficult to get the job at hand done if we always have to get the karma broom out of the closet.

I saw a bumper sticker once that I have since found out is a quote from Wayne Dyer: "How people treat you is their karma. How you react is yours." Very true. You can teach yourself how to avoid the karma quicksand by stepping back and being aware of the trap. It's all part and parcel of leading a mindful life.

Questions about Reincarnation

I have found that the subject of reincarnation is the one topic that interests the widest variety of my students. When I travel, I am always solicited for answers, and interestingly, the same questions are asked in various countries throughout the world. So, I thought this would be a perfect place to answer them.

Now, my insights may be different from what you've heard or what you accept in your heart, so if what I say feels right, take it in as food for thought. If it doesn't resonate with you, think about it and continue your research. Either way, I hope it stirs up a sense of curiosity on your part.

Why Don't We Remember Past Lives?

I believe that as the soul merges into the new physical vessel that it will occupy, it goes through what the mystic tradition refers to as the sea, or veil, of forgetfulness. Souls are meant to come into the physical dimension with a clean slate to start all over again. If a soul were to remember every poor choice and situation in the past, it would be so obsessed with how it did or didn't behave—or how it even destroyed lives—that this would influence the choices it made in this lifetime, and the soul wouldn't be able to concentrate on the current lessons it needs to complete. I do believe that all these memories are indeed accessible through our subconscious, but the conscious mind is what allows us to focus on this life. Otherwise, our heads would be so full that we wouldn't be able to function. Hypnosis and meditation are tools we can use to tap the subconscious if we feel that it would be helpful to review a past life.

What Determines When a Spirit Will Reincarnate?

As you can imagine, there are many factors involved in the choice for the soul to come back. Ideally, the soul will pick an opportunity that will present the greatest amount of learning, experiences, and scenarios for its optimal growth. This will most often be a combination of karmic obligations with other souls; various destiny points, challenges, or lessons; and of course, what will be the ideal social climate, family situation, and abilities afforded the soul with regard to its skills and gifts.

How Often Do We Reincarnate?

Remember that the soul always has free will. It can reincarnate if it chooses to, and it doesn't have to. There are many souls who do not *have* to come back to Earth, but decide to do so in order to help other souls in their growth. It is entirely the choice of the soul. Souls are able to evolve on the other side of life as well, but the challenges might not accelerate growth as quickly as those here on planet Earth. As a general rule of thumb, I've found that those souls who die young as children tend to come back more quickly. Those souls who have lived long lives on Earth tend to spend more time in the in-between stages.

Does a Soul Know What Its Circumstances Will Be on the Earth (Such as Adoption, Violence, Addictions, or Family Problems) Before the Incarnation?

Yes. Prior to returning, the soul sees the human life laid out beforehand so it is well aware of all the opportunities, challenges, possibilities, and choices likely to occur during its lifetime. But once the soul goes through the veil of forgetfulness and merges with the physical, free will plays a huge part in how that life will unfold. Following the path of love is always your soul's true desire.

Do Soul Mates and Soul Groups Reincarnate Together?

Yes—soul mates and soul groups are infinite beings who help you learn life lessons. Many of these souls have incarnated together and also inhabit the same spiritual realms. These souls are always in constant communication (whether incarnate or discarnate) and will work out the best and most opportune incarnation for all of them to be a part of so that the most karmic obligations and lessons can be fulfilled. These souls reincarnate together multiple times.

Do Human Spirits Ever Come Back as Animals, or Vice Versa?

I used to not believe this to be true, but then I realized that I was limiting the soul. Spirit is in all things, and there are lessons to be learned in all forms of existence. People think of reincarnating as the soul of a dog as a step down. Quite the contrary, if you think about it. For instance, aren't dogs just a true expression of unconditional love?

Why Would a Soul Choose a Body with Physical or Mental Challenges?

It is all about learning and having opportunities to grow. Perhaps the soul is living through a karmic lesson, or it may even have chosen this situation to teach others in its group about patience, compassion, and love.

Remembering Past Lives

Dr. Ian Stevenson wrote several books about reincarnation, most notably concerning the spontaneous recall of previous lives by children. I personally consider him a genius and pioneer who won't be recognized as such until long after his death (which occurred in 2007). The connection of the soul to the Spirit World in young children is still so fresh and new that recollections from a previous incarnation are present in the conscious mind. Children don't have the filter that comes with age and societal restrictions—they just say what's on their minds, even if it's viewed as impossible or crazy.

I find many of the stories I have read to be extremely compelling proof of previous lives. And I don't think the experience is limited to children. Have you ever traveled somewhere you'd never been previously but felt an odd connection to the place, sometimes even knowing geography or landmarks?

This happened to me many years ago when I was in my early 20s. I was driving with my friend John from Florida to California. We made a last-minute decision to stop along the way in New Orleans. I had no knowledge of the city other than having heard about Mardi Gras and jazz and great food. When John drove into the French Quarter, I began to have the strangest feeling in the pit of my stomach—a feeling that I *knew* this place. After John parked the car and we started to walk around, I confided in him about the eerie "knowingness" that I was experiencing.

John thought I was crazy, and so did I. (This was long before I had acknowledged my psychic gift.) It felt so familiar to me, and I knew every single street and alleyway. I knew where various churches and landmarks were located and also what buildings were connected to each other by underground passageways and tunnels. We never needed a guide map.

What *was* that? I'd never physically been there in this lifetime, but my soul obviously had experienced this location before, and because I knew specific hidden escape routes, it tells me that the lifetime would have been one where I would have had to use them.

In my work, I often hear of people having similar experiences, including ones where they have an overwhelming love for a particular type of food or nationality, or where they have an in-depth knowledge and understanding of specific historical events. They may also feel a attraction toward a culture, language, or part of the world. The soul always "remembers," and sometimes those memories bubble up from the subconscious to the conscious.

How many times have you met someone for the first time and sensed an immediate connection? This happened to me (again in New Orleans, but on a subsequent visit). Brian and I took a trip with a group of friends. I had an immediate connection with one of Brian's friends I had never met before, Ken. We later found out that we not only share the same birthday but are both fascinated by World War II, especially anything concerning Nazis or the death camps. We watch documentaries together on the subject and have even made a trip to Dachau. (You'd think Brian, whose great-grandparents emigrated from Germany, would have at least a passing interest in the subject, but he's not at all compelled.) Do I think Ken and I shared a life in World War II Germany? You bet I do.

On the flip side, you may also meet someone and feel an immediate dislike or mistrust and prefer not to be around him or her. Chances are that you have shared a previous life with that person, and the circumstances might not have been chummy.

I've heard of many instances where people have seen historical movies, like *Braveheart,* and felt an immediate emotional impact, as if they were watching a film about their own lives. This happened to me when I was watching *Glory.* It depicted various battles in the Civil War, and at one point I had to leave the theater because I had an overwhelming feeling that I would get sick if I watched any more. It was so palpable that when someone in the movie was bayoneted, I felt as if it were happening to me at that time. Dr. Stevenson recounts several instances where current-lifetime birthmarks appear in the area where a person had been wounded in a previous life.

Prodigies, Savants, and Doppelgängers

We've all heard of child prodigies—children who display astonishing skills for someone of their life experience. To me, a child who plays a Beethoven sonata skillfully at the age of three demonstrates that something else is going on. I'm also fascinated by the *savant* syndrome. This is a term used to describe people who have some kind of cognitive challenge but exhibit extraordinary ability in a specialized field such as mathematics or music. Is it the sole product of physical brain function, or is it the subconscious mind overtly working in tandem with the conscious mind? Dr. Stevenson also claimed to have studied children who exhibited *xenoglossy*—a phenomenon in which a person (usually under hypnosis) has the ability to speak in a foreign language that he or she has never been exposed to in this current life.

My friend Dr. Brian Weiss is the current leading expert in the use of past-life regression to help alleviate irrational fears, phobias, and habits. (His book *Many Lives, Many Masters* is a classic in the genre.) Dr. Weiss sees a direct correlation between unresolved past-life experiences and current-life phobias that interfere with his patients' everyday lives. An irrational fear of heights, water, close quarters, or being alone—or even the emotional fear of a relationship—could have its origin in a previous existence. Using hypnosis, past-life regression can bring that memory to the surface, where doctor and patient can calmly examine it and resolve the negative imprints. It can free the soul memory of this negative experience and aid healing on many levels. Dr. Weiss, like Dr. Alexander, is a respected physician and had much to lose and little to gain by telling his story and following his path.

There are websites now devoted to celebrities who have an uncanny resemblance to someone from the past. I don't put a whole lot of credence in them since everybody has a doppelgänger walking around somewhere. However, I do believe we can carry over similar physical traits from life to life, and I'll tell you a story that sealed the deal for me. Brian is the one who actually turned me on to the story of Helen Keller, and he's been fascinated with her since the fourth grade. (One of his prized possessions is an autographed photo of Helen that hangs above his desk.)

He was reading a biography of Helen recently. The book included a picture from the 1850s of Samuel Gridley Howe, a physician whose interest in helping blind children sowed the seeds of the Perkins Institution, which is where Annie Sullivan traveled from in Boston to meet Helen in Alabama for the first time. Brian had heard of Dr. Howe but had never seen his likeness before. It was like looking into a mirror for him. (If you're curious to know what Brian looks like, do a web search for Samuel Gridley Howe. They're identical except for the bad 1850s haircut.) Some people may say this is coincidence, but I say *coincidence* is God's way of remaining anonymous.

Remember the great 1993 comedy *Groundhog Day*? In it, Bill Murray plays an arrogant TV weatherman who keeps waking up to live the same day over and over again. At first he indulges in childish behavior knowing that the consequences won't matter. When he loses interest in that, he starts to transform his behavior and do good deeds and help people. When he finally gets the day just right, he is able to wake up on February 3.

Although the story doesn't involve reincarnation per se, the theme is very much the same. We, as souls, are given lifetimes filled with opportunities to learn and grow. We stumble and fail and try again, but we learn each time. And then with love as our guidepost, we finally get it right.

PART III

HOW THE SOUL LIVES IN THE PHYSICAL

CHAPTER SEVEN

‖‖‖

YOUR SOUL'S LESSONS

As souls, we are infinite beings with unlimited potential who inhabit a physical body on the earth to learn lessons about creating love. Our subconscious contains a plethora of soul experiences gleaned from a multitude of past lives, as well as the knowledge and wisdom of the Spirit World.

We utilize these remnants of cosmic wisdom to assist us in our next sojourn on planet Earth. The human world is one of the more difficult dimensions, because this is where the high vibration of *concepts* and *ideas* takes on physical form and is brought into reality. We aren't given an instruction manual at birth, so sometimes we don't know how to manifest these high ideals. Therefore, when we return to Earth, we must rely on the soul's innate "knowingness" or intuition to assist us in the optimal way to approach our human challenges and opportunities. We work through these lessons in the hopes that they will act as signposts to help our souls remember their ultimate destination and keep us on the right track.

Relationships

In this school called life, we will take various classes, which involve subjects or experiences we signed up for while still in Spirit. Before our incarnation, we choose the life we think will afford us the best opportunities and/or challenges to help us hone our skills in practicing the energy of love. For most souls, much of the curriculum is defined by the relationships they will experience on Earth. These relationships will present opportunities to learn valuable lessons that the soul wouldn't receive any other way. Therefore, *relationships* are the cornerstone of a soul's growth and learning. Earth is like a smorgasbord, offering a range of lessons the soul is seeking to perfect.

Soul Groups

Fortunately for us, we never go to school alone. Not only do we always have a constant connection to our tutors and guides, we also incarnate with "soul groups." The soul group will interact on Earth as family, friends, and lovers.

We've all heard the saying "You can pick your friends, but you can't pick your family." Well . . . yes and no. You've all picked each other as a well-thought-out cast of characters in a specific circumstance. Each member of this family has been through many past-life experiences together with you, developing an intricate pattern of energy that the group uses in order to learn and understand. If you're able to look at your family dynamic objectively (right now, as you're reading this), that insight can reveal the bulk of the lessons your soul has come back to learn.

Some families get along well and have more than likely learned the karmic family lessons of valuing and respecting each other. Dysfunctional families are still learning. These lessons are not always easy to master, because the people in your life who present the greatest challenges are usually your greatest teachers.

When you get into unpleasant circumstances with a member of your inner circle, don't jump into the emotion of the issue. Instead, step back, take a few breaths, and check your inner GPS. Love, forgiveness, and compassion are always the route to take, not judgment, retribution, and spite. Something else to consider when thinking of a challenging family member is whether perhaps he or she is holding a mirror up to you. Do you share the characteristics of someone who angers you?

Because we truly are connected as one, the elements demonstrated to you by family members represent what you must learn about yourself. For instance, perhaps you must learn about forgiveness or acknowledging your worth. There is no longer time for you to avoid, blame, or place judgment. If these lessons aren't learned, families find themselves revolving in a vicious cycle of disharmony. It takes great strength and perseverance for a soul to pull the family out of this chaotic, toxic energy so that everyone can view the situation from a higher perspective, learn the lessons, and begin to heal. You must also take into account that the healing may not just be for the benefit of the soul that is going through it, but it may also be an opportunity to heal *generations* in a lineage of imbalance and disharmony, resulting in tremendous advancement for the soul family.

As we all know, relationships can be the most intense and demanding of all the experiences we will go through in life, but also the most gratifying and rewarding. And since the energy of love is the ultimate vibration the soul seeks, relationships present us with the best opportunity to learn and explore it. But it's also important for us to *learn how* to love correctly.

Of course, the first step in building healthy, loving relationships is to learn to love yourself. You must accept yourself as a loving representation of Spirit if you're to accelerate your soul's earthly sojourn.

Everybody makes mistakes—everybody loses their temper; everybody judges—but if we make a conscious effort to be mindful every day of how we treat ourselves and others, life becomes much easier. One of my favorite Helen Keller quotes is "The unselfish effort to bring cheer to others will be the beginning of a happier life for ourselves."

Love Relationships

Intimate connections between two souls who are drawn to each other and share their lives as partners or a married couple are brought together because each one has an aspect of his or her soul makeup that the other partner might need to learn from. I personally am married to a man who I feel is one of the sweetest and genuinely pure souls that I've ever met. He is patient and kind, and in the 20 years I've known him, he has never said a bad word about anyone. If I come home and am upset that someone has behaved badly or inappropriately, he can always calm me down. He reminds me that I have to see the world from the other person's perspective before I can gain insight into that individual's motivation.

He is right. His favorite book and movie is *To Kill a Mockingbird,* and he believes that this is the overall theme—you need to walk around in someone's shoes for a while before you can truly understand that person. That's why the story resonates with so many people. We have even named one of our dogs Boo Radley, after the iconic character who is so misjudged and misunderstood.

Partners really assist us in finding within ourselves the *truth* that is there but maybe we haven't taken the time to acknowledge or express. Brian and I were drawn together because I am here to learn the insights that he has already gained: he is helping me understand and see things in a different way and without judgment. I am an outgoing extrovert who loves to laugh, and I am teaching shy, introspective Brian to enjoy life and people more. It is truly a pure balance when one soul-family member can contribute to another's growth and create a beautiful life together. You know when you share this bond because, besides your familiarity with each other, you become one being . . . one soul. The best in you finds the best in the other person.

Friendships

Just as important to our soul lessons as family and intimate partners are the relationships we create with friends. It is said that a person rich in friends has the greatest riches of all.

My good friend Joerdie Fisher is fond of saying, "You have a friend for a reason, a season, or a lifetime." We attract to us those energies that we need, and for however long we need them. In the Spirit World before our incarnation, soul groups plan out how they can assist each other in the next incarnation and what valuable lessons they can bring and share with each other, and it might last a week or many years. It can take lifetimes to develop close friendships, and the elements of trust, honesty, respect, and appreciation are worked on and worked out until the souls are in complete harmony with each other. Friendships are one of the greatest ways to express love.

"Like attracts like" is the Law of Attraction. If we live mindful lives centered on love and nonjudgment, we'll attract the same type of people into our sphere. If we give that energy out, those who also give out that energy will be drawn to us. If we're bitter, envious, and spiteful, we will not only draw those same people to us, but we'll repel the ones who can probably assist us the most in our souls' growth. Who would *you* rather have in your life?

When I teach my workshops and the students leave with a new sense of themselves as spiritual beings, they feel completely changed and more *centered* in themselves. I can actually sense their vibration shifting into a higher gear. And when these students who have been enlightened and empowered go home to friendships and relationships, they may discover that they're no longer in tune with some people in their lives. Career changes, location moves, and reevaluation of relationships are very common.

Once we are awakened to our life lessons and put them in proper perspective, we hopefully will gain a sense of mindfulness. We're more in control of our lives, and we make better choices with respect to how we interact with everyone in our sphere. We become aware of approaching life from a place of love and not fear. We begin to truly live in the moment. We are conscious of living from the *heart* space of compassion and understanding instead of the rational *head* space of criticism and judgment. From the *heart* space, we also are able to see other souls as being products of *their* life experiences and choices, and it's easier to empathize. By changing ourselves and our perspectives, we change our value systems and lifestyles. We are quickening our vibration and frequency to a higher level, and in turn, those around us begin to change. Love is the fastest vibration, so when the soul begins to work within this frequency, it changes not only us but our entire atmosphere and environment. As we rise in vibration, *all* of our relationships will change because *we* are changing.

There is a little-known Woody Allen movie called *Another Woman* in which Gena Rowlands plays a philosophy professor and author who operates so much from the left-brain, analytical side of herself that she is blind to the cold, emotionless exterior she presents to those around her. She feels superior and thinks that her blunt judgment of others is for their benefit. Her relationships have no depth, and she is comfortable keeping people at a distance. When she rents a quiet apartment in which to write her next book in peace, she realizes that through the air duct of the building, she can hear the raw, honest feelings of the patients in a psychiatrist's office next door. She is riveted by the authentic emotions of real people, and as she learns to accept her own personal shortcomings, her façade eventually starts to crumble and she begins the journey to transform her life. I think it's brilliant.

Specific Soul Lessons

I know that as you're reading through this chapter, you're attempting to grasp the specific lessons *your* soul is learning, and wondering if that is even possible. The answer is yes! But you must take the time to find the answers. Looking inward is the key, and the easiest way to accomplish that is through meditation. Depending on the intention behind your meditation, you can gain knowledge and enlightenment.

To gain insight into your soul's lessons, quiet your mind; take several deep breaths; and in your mind's eye, go back to a positive, joyful experience in your childhood. When you revisit this scene, live it and experience it as if you were part of it again. This is your starting point. (Remember, we are not going to be judgmental in our assessments; just come from a place of observation.)

Live in that experience fully, and feel the happiness. Now, slowly begin to see your life continue to unfold each year. Become mindful of the most important people in your life through these very specific times. Become aware and mindful of which people and situations make a strong emotional impact on you. Eventually you are going to bring yourself up to the present day. As you look back and experience your life, what specific scenes, situations, and behaviors seem to recur? Are you aware of the same experiences and your reactions to them repeating themselves? Do you sense that the major characters in your life have been cut from the same cloth? By being honest in your assessment, you identify the repeating themes or scenarios you experienced that are the lessons your soul has come back to learn for understanding and enlightenment.

Throughout my career, I have found that there are several recurring challenges that my students have acknowledged as repeating themes in their lives. I have compiled a list of the most common, and also the possible soul lesson that may correspond to that life experience. It can be incredibly insightful and helpful to choose a challenge from this list that resonates with you and use the corresponding lesson as a daily mantra.

Abundance

Lesson: Focus on what you do have instead of what you lack, because what you focus on is what you will receive. Know that you are a limitless being, and you are able to manifest whatever you desire.

Abuse

Lesson: You cannot control what happens to you as a child, but you do have the power to release the anger and feelings of betrayal. The karmic cycle of abuse is one of the strongest there is, and you must learn to break it with forgiveness and understanding.

Addiction

Lesson: The human body can be genetically predisposed to addiction. You have chosen this human vessel for a reason. You must learn that moderation and balance are the keys to harmonious physical, emotional, mental, and spiritual health. You must learn to accept the help of others.

Change

Lesson: New soul adventures and opportunities for growth cannot happen in a stagnant environment. Know that you are always safe and protected when outside your comfort zone.

Envy

Lesson: Comparing yourself to others is a learned trait, and it will deplete your innate happiness. Treasure and love yourself, because you never really know what personal obstacles others may face.

Failure

Lesson: Mistakes are the best way to understand your strengths and weaknesses, but they will bear fruit only if you acknowledge them and view them as opportunities to learn, instead of defeats.

Family

Lesson: Your soul partners have agreed to travel with you on this current journey. They are here to support you and help you learn. If your family seems more like a challenge, examine the dynamics objectively and make peace with what you are able to.

Fear

Lesson: Your priority in this life is to connect to the Source energy of love. Fear, in its many guises, is here to test you. Surrendering to fear only limits you and makes your path more difficult. Know that fear is an illusion and a trickster and that there are tools to help you resist it.

Forgiveness

Lesson: The ability to truly forgive is the richest tool of your soul. By releasing the negative energy that has been attached to you by the free will of another, you are unburdened of emotional stress and are breaking a strong karmic cycle.

Grief

Lesson: Something given to you and then taken away is an opportunity for you to appreciate having had it at all. Nothing is gone forever; loss is a powerful learning tool, but know that it is only temporary.

Guilt

Lesson: This emotion is one of fear's most devious guises because it is usually self-imposed. Forgiving yourself (and apologizing if necessary) is the "kryp-tonite" to neutralize guilt.

Health

Lesson: To nourish, maintain, and constantly assess your physical health is a priority and necessity if your soul is to be productive on Earth. An imbalance of your physical, emotional, or mental health is a challenge to spiritual growth.

Judgment

Lesson: Everything you see is made of the energy of Spirit. When you judge something, you are judging yourself. Everyone and all events you encounter on your path are here for a reason; learn to not label them as *good* or *bad*. They just *are*.

Relationships

Lesson: The souls you choose to have an intimate re-lationship with are your best teachers. They hold a mir-ror up to you and let you know what you are lacking. Your soul calls into your orbit those who will instruct you the most.

Self-Esteem

Lesson: The path that your soul has chosen will present you with obstacles that may deflate your sense of worth and confidence. You must learn that you are here to overcome and will succeed in all that you desire, and that any feelings of inferiority are merely an illusion.

The world can often seem like a very lonely place. It's important to remember that we are never alone. People (and even animals) can be placed in our path if we just lift our eyes from our cell phones and laptops and look around.

Your soul family on Earth is here with you, and your connection to everything you see is constant. Even if you're alone in a room, the love you're receiving from Spirit can be overwhelming if you open yourself up to it. There are a finite number of humans on this planet, and you are one of them. You are special. You are here for a reason.

CHAPTER EIGHT

SOUL CHOICES

The soul always has free will. It has the choice to expand and grow in Spirit, or it can choose to merge with the physical. When the soul demonstrates its free will on Earth, it can change the course of its own human life, the lives of those around it, or even the whole planet.

The choices we make are a huge responsibility, because even the little things that we do in life can impact many. So the soul is not only responsible for its own optimal growth; it is also accountable for its personal influence on every single thing—other humans, animals, and nature and the environment. In order for the soul to truly grow, it must align itself with its inner truth and make a conscious effort to be *mindful* every single day. But that takes practice.

Some people who have come to this awareness are better at it than others, but no one is perfect. When you reach this awareness in your soul's evolution, there will come a time for you to explore the road of self-discovery. Upon this road you'll soon realize that your current state of affairs has been created based upon the choices you've made in the past. At this pivotal moment you realize that although you've been impacted by the free will of others, you are completely responsible for the present *you*.

Love vs. Fear

Humans need to understand that life is a series of choices; we make them every single minute of every day of our lives. Some are mundane and some are substantial, but they *all* design our world. And the easiest way to make a choice is to ask ourselves whether our decision is coming from a place of fear or a place of love.

When I discuss this topic in my workshops, people look at me like I've lost my mind! It just seems too simple, and they try to rationalize reasons and excuses for not accepting the premise that all the important decisions we make in our lives can be linked to these two motivations. Most people overanalyze major decisions and make charts or lists with pros and cons—and there is nothing wrong with that. Or they do the opposite and just leave it to chance, or "let the chips fall where they may."

This is also a very relatable way of handling decisions because of the chaotic world we live in. All around us there is unconscionable violence, disrespect for life, economic uncertainty, degradation of the environment, and incredible poverty. We have to constantly remind ourselves that we may not be able to control the world and its problems, but we do have control over our microworld and our choices, with the hope that through sound, love-based decisions, we not only make *our* lives better but make the world at large a better place.

A well-respected colleague of mine, Marianne Williamson, says, "Love is what we were born into, and fear is what we learned here." This statement could not be any truer. Love is the soul's nature, and fear is foreign to it. So imagine expressing and living your life through an emotion that is not even natural to it, not even part of its inherent composition. It's like constantly paddling a canoe upstream, instead of going with the flow of love, which is the natural energy of the Universe.

Evaluating Your Choices

One of the exercises I use in my workshops to help people evaluate this truth is to have them review the major choices that they've made to bring them to this present point in life.

- Were they choices that your family urged you to make?

- Were they choices based on how you would be judged by others?

- Did the choices involve solely financial gain?

- Did you make choices because you wanted to win someone's love or acceptance?

- Or, did you make your choices based upon what you truly felt deep in your heart would be right for you—what would make *you* happy?

I then have my students review each major life choice, what motivation was behind that decision, and what the end result was. Most people find that the decisions they made from their hearts instead of their heads ended positively. I'm certainly not advocating that you jump into a decision without analyzing it, but if you let fear control your motivations, you usually won't end up happy.

Even if you attempt to make a life choice from a place of love, the possibilities can seem overwhelming. This can easily make you feel confused and out of control, and you may place conditions on your decision making. For example, if you were given the job of your dreams that encompassed everything you ever wanted, but it meant that you would have to relocate to a foreign city, what would your thought process be? Would it be that the challenges of living in a different country, learning a new language and culture, and leaving your family and friends would outweigh the prospect of a job that would make you creative and happy?

There is no right or wrong answer for everyone, but there is a right and wrong answer for *you*. Only you know what would make you truly happy, and you can make the decision easier for yourself by "following your heart." If you make choices based totally on love and what is right for you, then most become "no-brainers."

But if you make them based on fear or someone else's expectations, then chances are, you'll be swimming upstream trying to reach an ideal that never really was your goal.

Because the soul's true nature is love, if we stray from that motivation, we will never feel at ease. Choices based on fear leave us drifting aimlessly, always in search of our hearts' desires and never finding them. The symbolism of the final scene with Dorothy and Glinda in *The Wizard of Oz* is unmistakable. Dorothy comes to the realization that the power has always been within her to make the right choices; no one could make them for her. After acknowledging the power of her thoughts, listening to her heart, and gaining the courage to use these tools, she has the awareness she needs to overcome the challenges on her winding path and is finally able to go home: to the energy of love.

Listening to Your Soul's Voice

Choices always come with consequences. We have to accept the realization that ours may create situations that we never expected. Sometimes when we make a choice from a place of love, the Universe will test our commitment to our decision.

You may find that after the choice, unforeseen events occur that can make you question yourself. You begin to rationalize: *What if I had done this? What if I had done that? This might not have happened.* It is in this panic-stricken environment that commitment to the path you've chosen for yourself is tested. This commitment can be to anything: health, abundance, relationships . . . you name it. You must trust your intuition, your soul's knowingness.

When you make a conscious choice to base your decisions on love, there is a major freedom that also comes with that. There's no more second-guessing or doubt. Yes, there will always be circumstances or events going on that you can do nothing about. Other souls have free will, and you have no control over that. You know, *life happens.* But if you stay mindful of your own actions and become consciously aware that your power lies in this present moment, you'll get so much more out of life than merely existing. You'll begin to not take things for granted. You'll quickly see the little elements of life that bring sincere happiness and joy. The little annoyances that seemed so important and flavored with drama won't be as prominent. There will be times when you question yourself and overanalyze, but if you stay clear and honest with respect to your intention, you'll eventually begin to transcend your doubts and enter a state of "inner peace." Your soul's voice becomes clearer.

This is truly how the soul is meant to survive in this world. It is absolutely possible to practice mindfulness in every aspect of your life—at home, at work, and in relationships. You are an energetic being, and if you vibrate with the energy of love, then you are in sync with your true essence.

Michelangelo is quoted as saying that he saw *David* in the block of marble and carved until he set him free. So, too, can we carve away at all that is not *us*. That is our challenge: to chip away at all the expectations and demands of the physical dimension, to reveal our real selves—beings of love that honor and acknowledge our true mission.

Intuition is your guide to help you make the correct choices in life. If it doesn't *feel* right, then it isn't. You'll also have physical cues to help you—goose bumps, gut feelings, and a heavy heart are all physical manifestations of your inner voice. I learned many years ago when I was developing my intuition to pay close attention to how my body feels, because it will always tell me what is right for me. When these physical manifestations happen to you, recognize, acknowledge, and remember the sensation. That is the feeling that you want to have with each choice, situation, and event that presents itself on your path. That is your soul's GPS, and it will tell you the right turns and wrong turns that you're making, if you're listening.

There Is Always Choice

Choices are creative expressions of our soul selves. Whenever a circumstance presents itself, we have absolute free will to give it more power or give it a 180.

If you're presented with anger, and you react with anger, then you're giving it life. If you're filled with resentment, then you're practicing resentment. The more fuel you give an emotion, the stronger it becomes. The more people who make the conscious choice to be happy and loving, the more that energy will permeate the world. Make the decision to practice positive thoughts and neutralize negative ones.

Whenever I am faced with a challenging experience, I first sense whether I have the power to defuse the situation. I can control my actions, but I don't have the ability to control others. The Serenity Prayer is a useful tool:

God, grant me the serenity
To accept the things I cannot change,
Courage to change the things I can,
And wisdom to know the difference.

By using these words, I bring myself into a peaceful mind-set that doesn't create space for anger or low-lying emotions to take hold. I look at the situation from an objective point of view and ponder, *What is my soul learning from this?* Of course, it isn't something that easily came to me. I had to practice this way of thinking every day. I've even gotten into the habit of making a game out of it.

For instance, let's say I have just taken an exhausting, ten-hour plane ride, and I'm checking into a hotel, and the staff person behind the desk isn't being attentive. The game begins. How will I *choose* to react? I could get upset, rant and scream, and ask for the manager. This would leave me, the staff member, the manager, and any innocent bystanders all upset and unhappy, and that is the energy I've set up and have to live with. I would also have to be mindful that the energy I'm creating will have ripple effects. The staff and manager may use my negative energy on other customers, employees, or even family members. And *I* would be the source because of how I chose to react.

Instead, the other choice I have would be to wait until they have straightened out their situation, smile, and gently share with them how tired I am from traveling and how much I'm looking forward to lying down. I'd engage them and call them by name. In this way, I'm creating good energy that will come back to me. It's so much easier than fostering discord and having to live with it.

For years I've been practicing this aspect of mindfulness, and I've felt so much more at peace with the choices I make. I'm not always perfect, but I make a conscious effort. I know that my reactions have consequences and that I'll have to own them. I'd rather own nice things.

Choosing to be mindful should be the cornerstone of anyone's belief system. If your belief in how the Universe works isn't prompting you to be a kind person, then perhaps it's time to rethink your belief system, because something is obviously not working for you. After you've practiced being mindful for a while, it just becomes *who* you are instead of what you try to do. It's like learning to play an instrument or learning a new language: the conscious choices meld into natural ones.

Positivity begets positivity; negativity begets negativity. Thoughts of health maintain your health; thoughts of abundance bring you abundance.

You are connected to everything, and the creative power of the Universe is *you;* never feel separate from it. You have the choice of how you want to live today. You are not defined by your past or by things that may have happened to you in the past. Without those experiences, you wouldn't be who you are today. Sometimes you can't have what is in front of you if you're not willing to let go of what's behind you.

CHAPTER NINE

LIVING A SOUL-FILLED LIFE

There is a proverb, supposedly from the Cherokee, that I love. It goes: "When you were born, you cried and the world rejoiced. Live your life in such a manner that when you die, the world cries and you rejoice."

We all have the power to leave this world a better place than we found it. Some people do it on a grand scale; others do it by simply being kind, compassionate, and empathetic or by following the Golden Rule: treating others as they'd like to be treated. It's such an easy concept but one that seems beyond the grasp of many.

Humans use the movement of planet Earth to define time: one full rotation on its axis is a day; one revolution in orbit around the sun is a year. In our three-dimensional world, time is a necessary device, and the hours, minutes, and seconds pass us by so quickly that before we know it, precious moments are gone, never to be repeated.

If you can just pause every once in a while and become mindful of the space, people, and events around you and take it all in, then one day you'll be able to look back on the life you lived and know that your soul has generously appreciated every moment you've experienced on your journey. This is the beginning of enjoying a "soul-filled" life.

One of the indications that you're following your soul's path (and not living a life based in fear) is when everything seems *easy*. When life is full of coincidences and synchronicity instead of obstructions and roadblocks, then you know that you're on the right track. In my life, this has proved to be true over the years and often appears in the strangest of ways. When it happens, I feel as if I am moving to the beat of the cosmic choir, and when I truly listen to my intuition, I don't feel controlled by the illusion of fear and its many minions.

Living in the Moment

As I write this, I've just returned home from a weekend of pure soul fulfillment in Zurich, Switzerland. I was truly living in the moment, and the Universe was unraveling a plan I sensed had been set in motion long ago. Telling the story with mortal words can't express the amount of joy and happiness I felt as I was living out this plan.

Ever since I was a child, I've always wanted to visit Switzerland. I don't know why it calls to me, and in all the traveling I've done in the last 30 years, unfortunately Switzerland had never been on the agenda. Then a friend of mine phoned me out of the blue to say that there was a group of organizers who were producing what was advertised as an International Mediumship Congress in Zurich, and would I be interested? Needless to say, I signed on immediately, and I was honored to be the keynote speaker on that Saturday evening. I was also invited to do a full-day workshop on Monday. I took the 12-hour flight on Thursday. All during the flight, my heart was singing, and deep inside my soul, I knew this was beyond *right*. A wish that my soul had longed for was about to be fulfilled.

I arrived very early on a Friday morning after the long plane ride and six hours of sleep. But I was so excited that it felt like I was a child experiencing Christmas morning. I've been to many cities of the world where I have felt the dread of a past life. As beautiful as Paris, Istanbul, and Saint Petersburg are, I knew that my soul's human life had come to an unhappy end in those cities. Not so with Zurich. It felt light and joyful, and I was happy to be there.

The organizers put me up at the Baur au Lac, one of the most elegant and luxurious hotels I have had the pleasure to stay in. The staff, the grounds, the rooms— everything seemed otherworldly. After I checked in and dropped off my luggage, I was out to see the sights, and I kept hearing in my head: *Watch for signs!* I knew my guides weren't warning me about traffic signs; they were encouraging me to be receptive to the signs of Spirit.

Brian doesn't travel with me much anymore since we got the dogs. It's not that we couldn't find a totally reliable dog-sitter and know that Boo and Maisey would be fine; it's Brian who has the issue. He's just not happy being away from them for any extended period. Like four hours . . . tops. So that leaves me with the luxury of inviting other soul mates, old and new, on my business trips. I had just taught a mediumship class in Dublin earlier that year and met a lovely woman named Antoinette Byrne, and I knew immediately that we would become friends, so I invited her to Zurich.

I was not sure of when I was to meet Antoinette at her hotel; all I knew was that it was sometime in the early evening. After sightseeing, I strolled over to her hotel about seven to pick her up for dinner. The front desk told me that she hadn't checked in yet. I thought that was strange—I imagined she would have arrived by now. I sat down on the stairs in front of the hotel and got out my cell phone to call her. Before I could push the first number, a taxi pulled up and Antoinette jumped out with a big grin, and we hugged. It was a long, silent hug; it felt like the world stopped for a moment to acknowledge the bond of two friends. We knew without even verbalizing it that as we met, our souls had stepped into some kind of an enchanting vortex, and we had a sense that this time together was orchestrated by the Spirit realms.

After she checked in, we hit the city. During my afternoon of sightseeing, I'd picked out a restaurant that looked quaint, so we strolled over to it, crossing a bridge as a gaggle of geese swam under it. It was like a fairy tale.

At the restaurant as we looked over the menu, she said, "You know, I'm a vegetarian."

I felt horrible; I hadn't even thought to ask. Overhearing us, the waiter came back and handed us a vegetarian menu—they specialized in vegetarian cuisine.

We spent the next morning checking out the venue where the mediumship event would be held, and we met some of the mediums who would be demonstrating over the weekend. Everyone seemed so thrilled and excited to be there.

Antoinette and I left to go back to my hotel, but we became lost. Every time we thought we'd gotten our bearings, we would turn onto a street that we didn't recognize. We became so disoriented that it was actually funny. As we were laughing, she asked a stranger if he could help us. He had white hair and blue eyes and was impeccably dressed.

Antoinette told him the name of the hotel, and he said, "Allow me to drive you; it would be easier." He not only drove us to the hotel, but he gave us a mini-tour of the area and made sure we understood the main thoroughfares. At the hotel, he actually got out to open the car door for us.

As he drove away, Antoinette and I looked at each other, and we both said, "Okay, that was an angel." I wouldn't know what else to call him. He was perfect.

When we got to my room, we discovered a vase containing two dozen long-stem red roses with a note that said: "Thank you for coming to Switzerland." No sender's name.

I looked over at Antoinette, who had sat down in a chair. Her face was blanched. "Are you okay?" I asked.

"Roses. Don't you remember the roses?" she said. She had to remind me that during the class I'd taught in Dublin, Antoinette's deceased mother had come through one of the students and delivered the message: "I am the one giving you the red roses." At the time, we didn't know what it meant, but now we did! Her mother had died at a young age, leaving Antoinette to raise ten of her sisters and brothers. This was her mother's way of coming back and thanking her daughter.

The weekend was filled with unexpected surprises and delights. At one point, we thought of buying bath salts for our hotel tubs, but it was a Sunday, and Switzerland being a Catholic country, everything was closed.

We turned a corner and there was a bath store— open. The manifestations were occurring hourly.

Finally, Antoinette turned to me and said, "What's going on? Are you an alchemist?"

I laughed at her funny choice of words and replied, "I guess it's just meant to be."

The whole weekend made me ponder the difference between fate, destiny, or some hybrid that involves pre-determination *and* the subconscious and conscious energies of the participants. I believe that the weekend was fated and that we did have the free will to create a good time or a bad time, but there was an extra ingredient that I couldn't put my finger on. It was the effortless enthusiasm and joy we both surrendered to that made our time together so special.

Take two kindred spirits, add a dash of fate, cover it with enthusiasm and joy, release expectations, and you get magic. It really *was* alchemy. But what was that mystery ingredient that I couldn't define? I decided that Antoinette and I were experiencing soul-filled lives, and I decided to analyze the concept.

Becoming Aware

A soul-filled life is being consciously aware that you're connected to the Source and trusting that events will unfold for you in a Divine order. You always have free will, but you're so in tune with your intuition—your soul's voice—that your free will always makes the best decisions.

When we begin to program our thoughts and our lives by using our souls' power or intuition and not the critical mind, then and only then can we be free to soar. We don't even have to think about it; we just have to be aware and alive. True wisdom comes from the soul, not the brain. When we cut off the soul by giving our power away to the ego part of ourselves, it's as if we're minimizing who we truly are.

When you start living in accordance with the soul, joy overtakes negativity, abundance overtakes limitedness, and peace overtakes chaos. It is *you* who can create transformation and draw to you the perfect circumstances, relationships, and situations that allow you to expand and grow.

The first step in a soul-filled life is to be *aware*. When you become more aware of the physical world around you, and how the power you possess through your conscious acceptance of your connection to Spirit can change it, a whole *new* world opens up. It can benefit you by giving you a better understanding of what motivates you and everyone else who plays a part in your soul's life drama. But where do you start if you decide to lead a soul-filled life? I've been practicing techniques that I'll share with you.

Sitting in Silence

Start each day by taking a few moments to sit in silence. And I do mean *before* your day begins; this is time-specific, but can be accomplished in minutes. Sitting in silence can be one of the strongest gifts you can give yourself, and it's different from meditation in that the latter is quieting the mind of thought, but this exercise is more goal oriented. There are actually conscious thought processes going on. In this space you can begin to be connected to your thoughts and how you feel about yourself at that particular moment. Be aware of what your approaching day will entail. Play through your mind the scenarios that are likely to occur and how you would best like to react. Watch your thoughts. Are they negative or positive in nature? When you have these thoughts, where do they originate?

You may also consider sitting in front of a mirror and looking at your face in silence. This is what you're presenting to the world. What do you see? Can you become aware of what expressions you make that can be seen as friendly and welcoming, or anxious and wary?

Begin to listen intently to your body. Do a mental scan; your body will always talk to you and tell you what's going on with it. You know how somebody will say to you, "I've been having this pain in my side," and when you ask how long it has been going on, the person answers, "I don't know"? Really? As you get to know the subtleties of your body, you'll also begin to become more aware of what part emotions play in how your body feels. I have no doubt that the emotion accompanying certain events and people can trigger a physical response. Think about alternative ways to handle these encounters that can rid your space of this energy.

As we become more aware of our bodies, we begin to also become aware of various behavioral patterns we fall into. How do we react to certain circumstances? Do we have repeating thought patterns? Understanding our emotions and what triggers them can assist us in transforming our responses and making better choices in our lives. When we start to observe ourselves in this manner, we open the door to self-awareness on so many levels. Once we're honest about our feelings and reactions, we can also become aware of our expectation levels. Are our expectations about ourselves and others realistic?

Being in the public eye, I personally have to deal with this issue, and I feel that *my expectation of others* is a repeating theme that I wrestle with daily. I often assume that people will behave in the same way I do. But you know what happens when you *assume:* you make an *ass* of *u* and *me!* I endured many sleepless nights, unnecessary confrontations, and a few meltdowns before I accepted that everyone operates differently, and if I go into a situation knowing that, I'm able to give myself the time to discern if this person is going to gel with me. And not everyone is, and that's totally fine; I just need to decide if this is someone I want in my life. It doesn't make him or her good or bad; it just makes that person good or bad *for me* at this present moment. My expectation level that I could get along with anyone was unrealistic. But by being honest about who I am and listening to my soul's advice, I give myself permission to make choices that are correct for me and in turn will sustain a more appealing, exciting, and soul-filled life.

As you become more soul-conscious, know who you are, and present yourself to the outer world authentically, you will find more joy, peace, and harmony within yourself and with the people in your sphere. You're not going to like everyone, and not everyone is going to like you. It's a statistical impossibility. So don't fret over it, and don't feel guilty or insecure about it. If changing those statistics is important to your personal life or your career, you can take steps to do so.

Positive, happy people attract positive, happy people. Make a conscious effort to pay attention to your thoughts and the energy you're giving out. It is easy to dwell on negative circumstances in your life, but it's also possible to try to program yourself so that every time you have a negative thought, you can spin it into a positive one.

Reclaiming Your Joy

Being joyful is essential in spiritual life. When I conduct seminars, humor and joy are vital parts of my authentic self. Some people are confused by my attitude, because they think that talking to the dead should be a somber, serious affair. I couldn't disagree more. It's a joyous, happy event! It confirms that our "departed" loved ones are not really gone and that the bonds of love never die. What could be sad about that?

Joy is our natural state of being, but living in this limited physical dimension bogs us down. It is natural and normal that we live happy and full lives. We should understand that all we will ever need to be joyful is inside of us; we just have to learn to find it. It's the most important thing that Spirit incarnates to learn, but unfortunately, it's not taught to us by our parents or in schools or most churches.

Here are some tips for you to practice in order to reclaim your joy.

Set Your Intention

Having a clear, positive intention for your day is the easiest way to raise your vibration. Make sure that your intention is clear, but don't feel guilty if you don't manifest it. Just like a pole jumper who fails to clear the bar, dust yourself off and try again. Your intention can be general, like *I want to be less judgmental today,* or it can be specific if you're concerned about a confrontation or decision that is in the offing. Always envision the outcome as a happy ending.

Be Steadfast

Joy needs to be embraced on a daily basis, so when you set your intention, be sure to follow through. Don't let others influence you or talk you into what they think is the correct path. Advice is fine, but the decision is yours and you must live with the consequences. It's always best to look back at a decision and know that you succeeded in approaching it from a place of love instead of fear. This life is too short not to be happy—only manifest those outcomes that will bring you joy.

Play Every Day

Every morning after our dog walk, Boo runs to find his ball to play catch. It is a daily ritual that has taught me so much. The big things in life demand so much of our time that we often forget about the little things that bring us joy. No matter what it is that you enjoy—reading, doing crossword puzzles, connecting with friends—be sure you carve out a section of your day to make yourself happy. If you're not happy, then the people in your sphere can sense it, and they will become unhappy. If you feed your soul, it remains healthy.

Assess Your Current Self

Check in with yourself several times a day and make sure you're fine. Look objectively at your current emotions and see if a person or situation is making you anxious. What's the best remedy for your uneasiness? You have the power to manifest the most satisfying result. You have the power to change the trajectory. A consequence is always the result of any action, and you have the ability to manifest the most joyful consequence possible.

Have an Attitude of Gratitude

Always attempt to foster an attitude of gratitude. Do your best not to dwell or focus on the things that you may not have, but instead, be grateful for the things you *do* have. Life always presents challenges; instead of looking upon them as obstacles, view them as experiences to learn and grow and ultimately succeed. Grief, hurt, and pain are physical tools that the soul can use as stepping-stones to enlightenment.

Hold On to Happy Thoughts

You're human, and you possess human thoughts that can be critical and judgmental. Make an attempt to nip those thoughts in the bud and replace them with positive ones. Negative thoughts harm the recipient, and they harm *you*. When a critical thought pops into your head, immediately think of something that brings you joy or laughter, and use those emotions to revisit the critical thought. Remember that love is the natural energy of your soul; flow with it, instead of fighting it.

Take Care of Your Body

Just as the deep-sea diver checks his equipment and maintains it so that he can have a pleasurable time beneath the waves, so too do we have to take care of and maintain our earthly vessels. The soul can't walk around and learn its lessons if we don't become aware of the needs of our human shells. Do your best to eat the right foods and get enough rest and exercise daily. I walk or run every day, and I find that music helps the time to go by. But my exercise playlist always contains uplifting songs with positive lyrics. Much like Robert Monroe's work with "learning while asleep," I try to feed my subconscious with happy words.

Create Your Belief System

There is no right or wrong way to find your path to joy and love. We are all different, so the beliefs that guide our journeys are going to be different. There is a lot of spiritual wisdom in the world, and some of it will resonate with you and some won't. Embrace the ideas that make you the best person you can be and allow you to treat others with kindness and respect. New insights will come onto your path every day; be willing to take them into your heart if they seem right for you, or give them back to the Universe if they don't.

Let Go of What's Weighing You Down

Every once in a while, we have to do a spring-cleaning of our lives. Look around at yours and see which situations, people, and limitations are holding you back from living your joy. If it's a situation, examine it objectively and create a trajectory to bring it to a more joyful place. If it's a person, you two might have to discuss the obstacles in your relationship that are troubling you. You are here on Earth to vibrate with the energy of love, and if something or someone is lowering that energy, it needs to be addressed.

When our human lives have come to an end and the silver cord is severed, the energy of Spirit that we call a soul returns to its natural home. Its natural home is a dimension of energy that our human brains can only define as love, but that *love* is much more than what we can comprehend down here in the physical. The soul looks back on its earthly sojourn and examines its choices and actions and thoughts in a loving, nonjudgmental objectivity that is known as a *life review*. The soul feels the pain of those it hurt and the regret of opportunities it missed, but it also feels the love that it gave out and the kindnesses that it showed. During the life review, the soul realizes that it had one main objective on Earth, and that is to love. Challenges are put in the way of that objective, and if we made a conscious effort to listen to the voice of our soul while on this physical journey, chances are we'll have a lot to be proud of.

There is a great movie made in 1991 called *Defending Your Life*. In it, Albert Brooks plays a regular guy who dies and goes to Judgment City. There, he meets another new arrival played by Meryl Streep. She's very kind and sweet, and you can tell that she's led a mindful life. Her life review (which in the movie is like a trial) is going to focus on just four days of her human life, which is very low by Judgment City standards. Albert's character, who lived a life of fear and insecurity, is scheduled to view nine days, which is not so good. The movie is funny and sweet and surprisingly wise.

You have the power *right now* to make the conscious effort to transform your life into one of love and joy. You have the power to take the tools you've learned in this book and elsewhere so that your life review is more like Meryl's and less like Albert's. Your soul wants it for you, your loved ones want it for you, and Spirit wants it for you. Sure, there are going to be challenges, but if you look upon them as things you've chosen for yourself to conquer, instead of things done *to* you to make you miserable, it makes the experience much more tranquil.

I hope that by reading this book, you have been given illumination on your soul's adventures here on Earth and that it has inspired you to consciously seek out the path to love. I have created some guided meditations for you in the last section of the book that will help you on your path inward.

All of us are navigating our own personal yellow brick roads. Some of us are still asleep in the poppy field; some of us remain content with the material pleasures of the Emerald City. Some of us still think that the Wizard is great and powerful and follow his arbitrary commands to curry favor, while others have seen the man behind the curtain and have become disillusioned or feel betrayed. For the rest of us, once we acknowledge that our hearts' desires lie in our own backyard—inside of us— we'll be closer to home. And there's no place like home.

AFTERWORD

I debated over the best way to end this book, and I suddenly realized that it had been staring me in the face the whole time I was writing. Recently, as I was cleaning out the garage, I found my old framed copy of the poem "Desiderata," which was given to me by my friend John, who made that first trip to New Orleans with me so long ago. I now have it hanging in my office, and it continues to be a source of inspiration to me.

Its authorship was a bit confusing, as many attributed the poem to an anonymous writer who had left it in St. Paul's Church in Baltimore in 1692. It was actually written in the 1920s by Max Ehrmann, and it was used in literature that was circulated by a rector of St. Paul's Church, which was *founded* in 1692—thus the confusion.

To those of us who lived in the 1970s, it seemed to be a ubiquitous wall hanging, and it was also a popular song of that decade. I recently put it up on my Facebook page and received more "Likes" for it than for anything I had ever posted. Many people commented either that they had never seen the poem before or that they hadn't read it in a long time.

The title of the poem has been translated as "Things to be desired," and Mr. Ehrmann, a lawyer, wrote it as a way to reconcile his business challenges with his spiritual longing. It certainly speaks to the theme of this book, since we are all Spirit beings presented with earthly challenges, doing our best to follow the right path throughout our souls' adventures. Safe and happy journeys to you.

Love,
James

DESIDERATA

Go placidly amid the noise and haste, and remember what
peace there may be in silence.

As far as possible without surrender be on good terms with
all persons.

Speak your truth quietly and clearly; and listen to others,
even the dull and ignorant; they too have their story.

Avoid loud and aggressive persons, they are vexations to
the spirit.

If you compare yourself with others, you may become vain
and bitter; for always there will be greater and lesser
persons than yourself.

Enjoy your achievements as well as your plans.

Keep interested in your career, however humble; it is a real
possession in the changing fortunes of time.

Exercise caution in your business affairs; for the world is full
of trickery.

But let this not blind you to what virtue there is; many
persons strive for high ideals;

and everywhere life is full of heroism.

Be yourself.

Especially, do not feign affection.

Neither be critical about love; for in the face of all aridity and
disenchantment it is as perennial as the grass.

Take kindly the counsel of the years, gracefully surrendering
the things of youth.

Nurture strength of spirit to shield you in sudden misfortune.
But do not distress yourself with imaginings.

Many fears are born of fatigue and loneliness. Beyond a
wholesome discipline, be gentle with yourself.

You are a child of the universe, no less than the trees and
the stars;

you have a right to be here.

And whether or not it is clear to you, no doubt the universe is
unfolding as it should.

Therefore be at peace with God, whatever you conceive Him
to be,

and whatever your labors and aspirations, in the noisy
confusion of life keep peace with your soul.

With all its sham, drudgery and broken dreams, it is still a
beautiful world. Be cheerful. Strive to be happy.

SOUL JOURNEYS

Guided Meditations

My mission in life is to teach people about awareness, mindfulness, and discovering the soul's voice within. No matter where in the world I go, I always encourage people to begin the journey within by *practicing* meditation. And it does take practice.

The Purpose of Meditation

Meditation is the art of focusing and calming the mind. People meditate for various reasons, and it has been shown to lower blood pressure, increase memory, decrease depression and anxiety, and create an overall feeling of happiness about yourself and the world in which you live. A great number of people try meditation at some point in their lives, but small percentages actually stick with it for the long-term. There are lots of reasons why: impatience, not enough time in the day, too many intrusions, or unattainable expectations.

Some people have a knee-jerk reaction to the word *meditation.* They think of Eastern religions or New Age hokum. My mother would have laughed at me if I'd told her that reciting the Rosary was meditation—or reading a book, listening to music, or daydreaming. Anytime your mind is lost in thought, it is in meditation. How many times have you been on the freeway and suddenly realized that your exit was a mile behind you? How many times have you watched a TV show and then had to rewind the DVR because your mind was somewhere else . . . or had to start the chapter of a book over again because even though you'd been reading, you hadn't been comprehending?

These are examples of spontaneous meditation, and we all slip into it so effortlessly, but when we sit down and *try* to meditate, then our minds become alive with shopping lists and soccer games and other obligations. That's where the practice comes in.

Meditation has been around since the beginning of thought. There are scholars who believe they have evidence that ancient cave paintings in Spain and France depict meditators as far back as 14,000 B.C. From the sages of old to modern gurus, and all across the globe, we have been told that meditation has healing powers: psychological, physical, emotional, and spiritual.

Where do you begin? First you have to examine your intention. What do you hope to get out of meditating? I know of people who describe themselves as atheists who meditate for the physical benefits, and I know of others who meditate for the spiritual benefits. Everyone can benefit—but what is your intention, and what do you hope to get out of it?

To me, meditation is a doorway to the soul. Through years of practice, I can go into meditation with a focus and a question and come out with an answer and a feeling of peace—the peace that I have asked my soul what is the best path for me to take—and the knowledge that my request has been granted. For this book, I have created and tailored several meditations and affirmations to assist you in your process of self-discovery on your path to love.

Meditation Preliminaries

When you decide on your intention, before any meditation or inner-journey experience begins, you should carefully choose the location and space you will meditate in. If at all possible, it would be ideal to designate a special place solely for this purpose because it not only places the intention into that space, but the meditative energy can build up over time. Also, when you enter this space, you automatically know that you're in the environment that you've chosen exclusively for this purpose, and in a way, it gets you ready to begin. If not, choose a quiet place that receives the least distractions and where you are comfortable. Preferably, it would be a room in your house or apartment or even a place in the garden that would not be used for any purpose other than some type of healing work.

You want a limited amount of outside distractions such as the phone, television, and radio. It is also very important that the space be kept neat and clean.

Remember that any location you are in affects the mind, therefore your environment should be one that is pleasing to you. Seeing and being part of a beautiful space makes the mind happy, and a happy state of mind is conducive to delving into your inner discovery.

I find that, even though you can meditate at any time, a formally set hour of the day will also assist in preparing your mind and reinforce that this is time you have set aside for this one and only purpose. This enables you to pick a time when you're least likely to have distractions, but it also demonstrates a certain amount of respect for the process.

I think it is also important that before you start meditating, you acknowledge that this is a personal journey, and although you may want to eventually assist others and/or share the experience, you will have to be very careful when sharing the space with another person. This is because other people can be a distraction and also because the energy that you have built up can be diminished.

After you have selected your space and you're confident that you won't be disturbed, put yourself in a comfortable position, with your back straight. You want the energy to flow freely up and down your body. Once you are comfortable, the first thing to do is become mindful of your breathing. Focusing on your breath can be very calming, much like the ticking of a clock or a metronome. Breathe normally through the nose, not too quickly, not too slowly, not too deeply, and not too shallowly. Do not hold your breath, but pause after each exhalation before breathing in again.

Focus on your breathing and become aware of how it clears your mind and slows your heart rate. Having your eyes open or closed is a personal choice, but if your eyes are open, you should be looking at something you enjoy. Many people have an altar for this purpose or a favorite image, like a mandala. Incense is also a personal choice, as is low music. You may need it to cover ambient sound like traffic or neighbors. Also wear comfortable, nonrestrictive clothing. Drink enough water so that you don't become thirsty during your meditation, but not so much that you feel the need for a bathroom break.

Let your mind relax and wander. You will no doubt have thoughts pop into your awareness, like your dry cleaning is ready or a term paper is due. Acknowledge the thought and let it go. This is only your conscious mind throwing a little tantrum and trying to get your attention to let you know that you have things to do. Put your conscious mind in its time-out corner and let it know that it doesn't need to worry—you'll be back soon. Your conscious mind gets more than its fair share of your waking awareness. Not only will it understand why you're putting it on the back burner; it will learn to enjoy its time there.

I have created a few guided meditations for you to get you started. You can read them over before you begin, or you can read the meditations into the voice memos of your phone or a tape recorder to play back during your session.

Your Soul's Sanctuary

Imagine yourself sitting in an ornate gold chair that has a red velvet cushion. You are alone in a room of complete and utter beauty, and soft sunlight is shining in the windows. A fire is burning in the fireplace, and it warms the room. The walls are made of stone that seems to shimmer, and when you look up, you can barely see the ceiling. There are several large oil paintings in the room, and you recognize them as significant locations from your life.

Walk around the room and take a long look at each painting. How does each location make you feel? Try to remember a cheerful time at each place. Lining the walls of this room are shelves, and they all contain framed photographs of you. Look closely at each photograph and acknowledge what age you are and who is in the photo with you. Each photograph is significant to you, and each photograph makes you happy.

The shelves also contain mementos of your life that you have cherished. Pick each one up and remember how important it was in your life. A flood of memories comes to you as you hold each object. One shelf holds several leather-bound books. Take a look at each title slowly. The titles are the different lessons that your soul has chosen to learn. Reflect on how you are performing each lesson.

Choose one of the books and carry it with you back to your golden chair. Open the book and, one page at a time, look at the photos inside. How old are you in the photo and who are you with? Are the photos telling you a story? What are you learning from the story? There is no judgment in this; you are merely looking and assessing.

When you feel that you understand what the book is telling you, gently close it and hold it to your chest. Look around the room and take it all in. Feel the love that the room is giving to you. The room loves to have you here. There is no hurry; you may stay in this room as long as you'd like. This is your home.

When you feel that it is time to go, take a few deep breaths. In your mind's eye, envision your meditation space back in the human world and see yourself sitting in that space. Take the love you feel in the sanctuary and fill your meditation space with it. Slowly become aware of your consciousness in the meditation space. Take a few deep breaths and slowly open your eyes.

Healing Your Soul Self

Imagine yourself walking along a tree-lined path. It is a beautiful, sunny day, and you can smell the fresh air. With each deep breath of this fresh air, you are walking closer and closer to the end of the path, which is an arbor covered with vines and flowers. The opening is beckoning to you. It seems brighter past the opening, and you can hear birds singing beyond it.

As you walk under the arbor, stop for a moment and become aware that your next steps will lead you into the dimension of Spirit. Continue walking and feel the warmth on your face from a sun so clear and bright that the meadow before you seems to glimmer. The trees are so full and tall that you can barely see the tops. Birds of all kinds fly above and call to each other. Slowly look around your garden and acknowledge everything. The rolling hills of the meadow disappear to the horizon, and animals of all kinds frolic in the shade of the trees. Flowers of every color have blossomed at your arrival, and butterflies dip and soar.

Look all around and absorb this view, and as you do, let your consciousness expand as far as you are able. Everything that you see is perfect; everything that you sense is at peace. A stream catches your attention as it sparkles in the sunlight. The water flows gently to a waterfall, which beckons you in. The water is warm, and as you stand under the falling water, a rainbow appears in the mist in front of you. The water seems to change to each color of the rainbow as you stand under it, and you can feel the energy of the human world wash off you.

Stay under the water until you feel as light as air. In fact, you are floating but with complete control. As you float up through the rainbow, you are afforded a view of the most beautiful tree that you have ever seen. As you glide effortlessly over to the tree, you realize that the tree is your soul. This tree is you. You instinctively know that the four main branches of the tree represent the physical, emotional, mental, and spiritual parts of you.

You are free to float among the branches and inspect what doesn't feel or look healthy. Ask the tree what is wrong; it will tell you. Embrace the branch of the tree that asks for help and infuse it with love. Watch the old leaves blow away with the wind and see the new fresh, green leaves appear.

The tree beckons you to sit among the branches, and as you do, you feel complete and whole. With your love, the tree glows with health, and flowers bloom in its canopy. The gratitude that you feel from the tree fills your heart with happiness, and you acknowledge that you will always be available for healing. You will always be together.

As you sit on the branch, enjoy how clean and light the waterfall has made you feel—you can actually see through your hands as you hold them up. Close your eyes and take a few deep breaths of the beautiful green smell of the tree and caress the healthy leaves that you have made. Picture yourself in your meditation space and infuse your body with all the happiness and gratitude that you felt on your journey. Take a deep breath and allow your consciousness to return to your physical body. When you are ready, slowly open your eyes.

Thanking Your Soul Family

Imagine yourself walking along a cobblestone street. There is no one in sight, and you are not aware of the location or decade, but you feel comfortable and relaxed and know that you are welcome. The sun has just risen, and it is going to be a beautiful morning.

Up ahead, you see that the street ends at a public square with a grand fountain. As you inspect the fountain, you admire the workmanship that has gone into it. You recognize the stone characters that adorn the fountain as people you have known in your current life. They all look happy and cheerful, and they are looking up to the central stone figure that is higher than everyone else. It is *you.* The statue of you has its arms raised high, and you are laughing. As you look at this visage of yourself, you cannot help but smile as the mist of the fountain lightly caresses your face.

You hear a door opening behind you, and you notice that what appears to be the village theater has opened. You walk over to it and go inside. The lobby is very ornate, and the jewels and gems in the walls cast prismatic reflections onto your face. The lone door of the lobby beckons you further inside. It is dark in here, but you see one chair facing the stage.

The stage is lit up and is covered by a purple curtain. As you make yourself comfortable in the chair, the curtain opens, but the stage is empty. Instinctively, you realize that it is up to you to invite someone from your life out onto the stage. It is up to you whom you would like to talk to. It can be your mother or father or spouse. It can be someone living or in Spirit. You sense that everyone you would ever want to talk to is waiting backstage and would love to see you. Everyone in your life wants you to understand why you were brought together in the physical.

Anyone whom you call out is aching to have a dialogue with you and comfort you.

When you make your decision, the person you want to talk to the most today appears from the wings. They are so happy to see you. They are waiting for your questions. They have answers for you. Everything that they say makes so much sense to you; you understand their motivation and you feel their love. No question that you ask will go unanswered. Your heart feels so light with the understanding of your physical journey together. You thank each other for the lessons that you both have brought to one another.

You may ask someone else out to the stage or save that discussion for your next visit to the theater. When your loved one walks offstage, you can see yourself in the middle of the stage. You are in your meditation space, and you are smiling. Fill that space with the understanding you have received from your dialogue. Take a deep breath and become aware of your consciousness returning to your physical self in the meditation space. As the curtain closes, close your eyes and feel yourself back in your body. Take one more deep breath and slowly open your eyes.

ACKNOWLEDGMENTS

My biggest thank-you goes to Brian Preston and our dogs, Boo Radley and Maisey Mae. Brian, thank you for being the rock and letting me be the kite.

Thank you to the following people whose souls have agreed to travel with me on this adventure: the Fortune family, the Barry family, the Opitz family, the Preston family, Mary Ann Saxon, Joerdie Fisher, Kelly Dennis, Kelley Kreinbrink, Jeff Eisenberg, Dorothea Delgado, Marilyn Whall, Doreen Virtue, Gabrielle O'Connor, Scott Schwimer, Jacqie Ochoa-Rosellini, Joe Skeehan, Teresa Griffin, Christian Dickens, Kellee White, Bernadette, Mavis Pittilla, Jean Else, Wesley Eure, Tori Mitchell, Randy Wilson, Ken Robb, Chip McAllister, Knute Keeling, Ron Oyer, the Kaba Family, Peter Redgrove, Cyndi Schacher, Roberta Kent, Antoinette Byrne, Lisa Malcom, Angie Lile, Kris Voelker, Katrin Hall, and everyone at Hay House.

ABOUT THE AUTHOR

James Van Praagh is an internationally renowned #1 *New York Times* best-selling author. He has written extensively about life after death, Spirit communication, grief, and healing; and his messages have brought solace, peace, and spiritual insights to millions, changing their views on both life and death.

James introduced the world to mediumship on the NBC daytime television show *The Other Side* in 1994. Since then, he has appeared on nearly every national radio and television program, including *Oprah, Larry King Live, Dr. Phil,* A&E's *Biography, Nightline, Unsolved Mysteries, The View, The Joy Behar Show,* the *Today* show, *Dr. Drew's Lifechangers, Chelsea Lately, Coast to Coast,* and many more. His international reach expanded even further when he hosted his very own daytime talk show, *Beyond with James Van Praagh.*

In addition, he is a successful producer in network television, with one of the most-viewed miniseries in CBS history, *Living with the Dead,* starring Ted Danson in a biographical portrayal of James; and *The Dead Will Tell,* starring Eva Longoria. He also co-created and produced the highly successful series *Ghost Whisperer,* starring Jennifer Love Hewitt.

James teaches workshops and classes and performs mediumship demonstrations throughout the world.

For more information, please visit his website: www.vanpraagh.com.

Hay House Titles of Related Interest

YOU CAN HEAL YOUR LIFE, the movie,
starring Louise Hay & Friends (available as a
1-DVD program and an expanded 2-DVD set)
Watch the trailer at: www.LouiseHayMovie.com

THE SHIFT, the movie, starring Dr. Wayne W. Dyer
(available as a 1-DVD program and an expanded 2-DVD set)
Watch the trailer at: www.DyerMovie.com

*HEART OF MIRACLES: My Journey to Life After a Near-Death
Experience,* by Karen Henson Jones (available February 2015)

*LOVE NEVER DIES: How to Reconnect and Make Peace
with the Deceased,* by Dr. Jamie Turndorf

PAST LIFE ORACLE CARDS, by Doreen Virtue and
Brian L. Weiss, M.D. (a 44-card deck and guidebook)

QUANTUM CREATIVITY: Think Quantum, Be Creative,
by Amit Goswami, Ph.D.

*THE SHADOW EFFECT: Illuminating the Hidden Power
of Your True Self,* by Debbie Ford (available as a 1-DVD
program and an interactive 2-DVD set)

*SOUL LESSONS AND SOUL PURPOSE: A Channeled Guide
to Why You Are Here,* by Sonia Choquette

*YOUR LIFE AFTER THEIR DEATH: A Medium's Guide
to Healing After a Loss,* by Karen Noé

All of the above are available at your local bookstore,
or may be ordered by contacting Hay House (see next page).

We hope you enjoyed this Hay House book. If you'd like
to receive our online catalog featuring additional information
on Hay House books and products, or if you'd like to find
out more about the Hay Foundation, please contact:

Hay House, Inc., P.O. Box 5100, Carlsbad, CA 92018-5100
(760) 431-7695 or (800) 654-5126
(760) 431-6948 (fax) or (800) 650-5115 (fax)
www.hayhouse.com® • www.hayfoundation.org

Published and distributed in Australia by: Hay House Australia Pty.
Ltd., 18/36 Ralph St., Alexandria NSW 2015 • *Phone:* 612-9669-4299
Fax: 612-9669-4144 • www.hayhouse.com.au

Published and distributed in the United Kingdom by:
Hay House UK, Ltd., Astley House, 33 Notting Hill Gate, London
W11 3JQ • *Phone:* 44-20-3675-2450 • *Fax:* 44-20-3675-2451
www.hayhouse.co.uk

Published and distributed in the Republic of South Africa by:
Hay House SA (Pty), Ltd., P.O. Box 990, Witkoppen 2068
Phone/Fax: 27-11-467-8904 • www.hayhouse.co.za

Published in India by: Hay House Publishers India, Muskaan
Complex, Plot No. 3, B-2, Vasant Kunj, New Delhi 110 070 • *Phone:*
91-11-4176-1620 • *Fax:* 91-11-4176-1630 • www.hayhouse.co.in

Distributed in Canada by: Raincoast Books, 2440 Viking Way,
Richmond, B.C. V6V 1N2 • *Phone:* 1-800-663-5714
Fax: 1-800-565-3770 • www.raincoast.com

<u>Take Your Soul on a Vacation</u>

Visit www.HealYourLife.com® to regroup, recharge,
and reconnect with your own magnificence.
Featuring blogs, mind-body-spirit news, and life-changing
wisdom from Louise Hay and friends.

Visit www.HealYourLife.com today!

Free e-newsletters from Hay House, the Ultimate Resource for Inspiration

Be the first to know about Hay House's dollar deals, free downloads, special offers, affirmation cards, giveaways, contests, and more!

 Get exclusive excerpts from our latest releases and videos from *Hay House Present Moments*.

 Enjoy uplifting personal stories, how-to articles, and healing advice, along with videos and empowering quotes, within *Heal Your Life*.

 Have an inspirational story to tell and a passion for writing? Sharpen your writing skills with insider tips from *Your Writing Life*.

Sign Up Now!

Get inspired, educate yourself, get a complimentary gift, and share the wisdom!

http://www.hayhouse.com/newsletters.php